255.532
F

255.53 FLE

W9-BYP-690

LIBRARY

Oct. '84

Near Manresa, Spain, which faces the lof...
the river Cardoner, St. Ignatius in 1522 ...
illuminations from God; and from the...
largely sprang (Autobiography, espe...

In these Exercises Ignatius...
St. Augustine had exclaime...
O Lord, and so worthy...
us to find delight in...
yourself, and our...
rest in you (Conf...

This book is No. 2 in
Series IV: Study Aids on Jesuit Topics

David L. Fleming, S.J.

A CONTEMPORARY READING

of the

SPIRITUAL EXERCISES

A Companion to St. Ignatius' Text

Second Edition, Revised

THE INSTITUTE OF JESUIT SOURCES
St. Louis, 1980

IMPRIMI POTEST: Very Reverend Leo F. Weber, S.J.
Provincial of the Missouri Province
January 19, 1978

IMPRIMATUR: Most Reverend John N. Wurm, S.T.D.,
Ph.D. Chancellor, Archdiocese of St.
Louis March 31, 1978

Experimental edition, 1976
Second edition, revised, 1980
Second printing, 1982

© 1978 The Institute of Jesuit Sources
Fusz Memorial, St. Louis University
3700 West Pine Boulevard
St. Louis, Missouri 63108

All rights reserved
Printed in the United States of America
Library of Congress Card Catalogue Number: 80-81812
ISBN 0-912422-47-5   paperback
0-912422-48-3   Smyth sewn paperback

CONTENTS

Contents

EDITOR'S FOREWORD

The little book presented here is an endeavor to present the substance or chief ideas of St. Ignatius' well-known *Spiritual Exercises* in language which modern readers can understand more easily and quickly than the saint's often difficult sixteenth-century text. In this way, hopefully, the book will be especially helpful to readers who are making a first acquaintance with the *Exercises*, for example, in a directed retreat, or in the "Spiritual Exercises Made during Daily Life" which are often referred to as "At Home Retreats" or "Nineteenth Annotation Retreats" according to *Spiritual Exercises*, [19].

Father Fleming gives us here, without any change in title, an enlarged revision of his first or "Experimental Edition" of 1976. To that he has added here his "readings" of Ignatius' Three Methods of Prayer, Rules for Distributing Alms, Notes on Scruples, and the directives commonly called "Rules for Thinking with the Church," all of which were lacking in that first edition.

Since 1976 the author has profited from many suggestions made by retreatants and directors who used his first edition, and also from his own experience with it. In June, 1978, he published an enlarged revision, entitled *The Spiritual Exercises of St. Ignatius: A Literal Translation and a Contemporary Reading*. In it he printed St. Ignatius' own text of the *Exercises* on pages opposite the corresponding contemporary readings. This facilitated achievement of one of his aims, namely, that this work would be a gateway to St. Ignatius' text rather than a substitute for it. This revision has received a warm welcome.

Nevertheless, many requests have continued to come in for the smaller and naturally less expensive work. When the publisher's stock of the experimental edition became exhausted, the decision was made to keep the small work available, not by a mere reprinting, but by using the revised and enlarged "Contemporary Reading" which had appeared opposite the text of St. Ignatius' *Spiritual Exercises* in the book published in June, 1978. This is the "Contemporary Reading" which the Institute of Jesuit Sources is now happy to offer in the present book.

George E. Ganss, S.J.
Director and General Editor
The Institute of Jesuit Sources
Easter, April 6, 1980

AUTHOR'S PREFACE

The present small book is intended to be a gateway to St. Ignatius' *Spiritual Exercises*, a means to make his widely renowned but difficult text more easily and quickly understood by contemporary men and women—especially by those using it for the first time in directed retreats.

The *Spiritual Exercises* of the founder of the Jesuits has been a classic retreat manual in the tradition of the Church for the past four hundred years. Spiritual classics, of their very nature, are not meant to be rewritten or tampered with.

Yet significant contributions to the understanding of the *Exercises* and its application in practice have been made throughout the centuries since the first publication of the book in 1548. During Ignatius' own lifetime and for the first fifty years after his death, various commentaries on the text of the *Exercises* were written which looked primarily to the actual practice in giving the Exercises and were called "Directories." After the official *Directory of the Spiritual Exercises* was promulgated by Father Claudio Aquaviva, General of the Society of Jesus, in 1599, there was something of a lull in this style of writing. But soon commentaries of different types—some more in the nature of theological explanation of the text, others still practice-oriented in terms of particular movements or devotions in the Church— were forthcoming. In our own more recent past, retreat manuals were written in which the conferences of a preached-style retreat were put into print so that they could both inspire other directors and help other retreatants. These books provided a certain understanding of the *Exercises,* and they also at times gave direction through the written word to those who made use of them for their own private retreats.

Today, the popularity of the directed retreat has led directors and retreatants back to the starkness of the original Ignatian text. But the text itself, despite a simplicity in style, presents difficulties in word expression, image patterns, terminology, and even in world view—for Ignatius' outlook on the world was a good deal more medieval than ours is. Often the director and retreatant of today spend time on technicalities of the saint's text—time which often could be better employed in the movement of the retreat itself. I believe that what might be helpful to people of our times would be an attempt to preserve the original sparseness of the Ignatian text, yet to express it in such a way that the book seems not quite so formidable for either the present-day director or the retreatant. I would hope that the director would find such a reexpression of the Ignatian text enlightening and opening into new depths of understanding. In a similar way, it is my desire to be able to provide a reading which the director would find is less forbidding in terminology and less tortuous in explanation when he wants to put the text in the hands of a retreatant. In other words, I want to present the text in such a way that it is as easily usable and understandable for people of today as Ignatius' text was for the people of his time.

This, then, is why I entitle my efforts "a contemporary reading of the *Spiritual Exercises*." It is not a translation in the more usual sense of the word, for I am not struggling with a rendering of the Spanish or Latin versions. Even though I have at times expanded and rearranged some parts of the text, I do not want this work to be considered a commentary or a substitute for the text of Ignatius; it is, instead, a way of "reading" Ignatius' own text.

In the enlarged edition published in 1978, I attempted to facilitate the movement between this "reading" and the original text of Ignatius by placing a very careful translation made from his Spanish autograph text by Elder Mullan, S.J. on the pages opposite to my own reading. For Jesuits as well as for many others long familiar with the original text, such an arrangement proved to be helpful for a closer working with the text both within the retreat context and outside of it for study purposes.

But experience has shown that many people are well served just by the "reading" alone, especially when it is used with the guidance and help of a retreat director. Therefore the present edition similar to the original preliminary edition of 1976 has been prepared by taking only the revised "reading," but in its entirety, from the enlarged edition of 1978. Thus the book remains small and inexpensive—and also, hopefully, easily available for the large numbers now making directed retreats, or retreats in the course of their ordinary daily lives (according to the manner indicated by Ignatius in his Nineteenth Annotation (*Spiritual Exercises*, [19]).

I am happy and grateful that so many directors and retreatants have found this "reading" of the Spiritual Exercises so helpful. It is a privilege to be able to share in a new way the richness of this spiritual classic with the men and women of today.

May St. Ignatius bless our efforts to know Jesus Christ a little more intimately so that we all can follow Him a little more closely.

David L. Fleming, S.J.
Epiphany, 1980

THE PRAYER "SOUL OF CHRIST"

Jesus, may all that is you flow into me.
May your body and blood be my food and
drink.
May your passion and death be my strength and
life.
Jesus, with you by my side enough has been
given.
May the shelter I seek be the shadow of your
cross.
Let me not run from the love which you offer,
But hold me safe from the forces of evil.
On each of my dyings shed your light and your
love.
Keep calling to me until that day comes,
When, with your saints, I may praise you for-
ever. Amen.

SOME PRELIMINARY HELPS

(from the reading of the

Spiritual Exercises, [1-20] *)

The purpose of these observations is to provide some understanding of the spiritual exercises which follow and to serve as a help both for the retreatant and for the director of the retreat.

A. *For the Retreatant*

1. The phrase "Spiritual Exercises" takes in all the formal ways we have of making contact with God, such as meditation, contemplation, vocal prayer, devotions, examination of conscience, and so on. We are familiar with the great variety of physical exercises, such as walking, jogging, playing games such as tennis, handball, golf, or even the demands of yoga and isometrics. These physical exercises are good for tuning up muscles, improving circulation and breathing, and in general for the overall good health of the body. So, too, what we call Spiritual Exercises are good for increasing openness to the movement of the Spirit, for helping to bring to light the darknesses of sinfulness and sinful tendencies within ourselves, and for strengthening and supporting us in the effort to respond ever more faithfully to the love of God.

2. In the Spiritual Exercises which follow, we find ourselves [3] sometimes doing much thinking and reasoning things out. At

---

*The numbers enclosed within square brackets, e.g. [3], refer throughout this book to the paragraph numbers found in most modern editions of *The Spiritual Exercises* of St. Ignatius of Loyola, which was first published in 1548. These numbers were first added to his text in the edition published in Turin in 1928, in order to make references easier. In this present *Contemporary Reading* by Father Fleming, *Spiritual Exercises* in italics refers chiefly to Ignatius' book, Spiritual Exercises in roman type to the activities within a retreat.

other times, we experience far more the response of our hearts, with little or nothing for the head to be concerned about. It is good to remember that we are always in the context of prayer, whether meditative or affective, and so we should always try to maintain a spirit of deep reverence before God.

[5]   3. The most important quality in the person who enters into these Exercises is openness and generosity. As a retreatant, my one hope and desire is that I can really put myself at the disposal of God so that in all ways I seek only to respond to that love which first created me and now wraps me round with total care and concern.

[20]   4. Ordinarily, if we want to give ourselves over to the movement of these Exercises, it is most helpful to go apart from what usually surrounds us—both friends and family, job and recreation, and our usual places of home and work. There are many advantages which come from this separation, for example: (1) if I am so intent on responding ever better to the love of God wherever it will lead me in my life, I will find the kind of quiet in which the movement of God in my life becomes all the more apparent; (2) my mind will not find itself divided over many cares, but rather its one concern will be to follow the lead of God; (3) in a similar way, my powers of loving, too, will be focused for this amount of time solely upon God, and the response which I will be able to make is all the more intense and intimate because the demand for such a response is so single.

[4]   5. The makeup of the Exercises is rather simple. The basic division is into four parts, called "Weeks," although there are no fixed number of days within these respective "Weeks." The First Week is set in the context of God's love and its rejection by each of us through sin. The Second Week centers on the life of Jesus, from its beginnings through his public ministry. The Third Week fixes upon that very special time of Jesus' life—his passion and death. The Fourth Week looks upon the Risen Christ and the world which has been renewed in his victory.

We move from Week to Week according to the grace which God gives to us. Some persons come to an appreciation of a certain mystery of God's dealing with themselves more rapidly than others. For each person, it is the director who determines whether the time of the Week should be shortened or lengthened according to the movements of God's grace and each one's ability to respond. We note, however, that the full Exercises should be completed in approximately thirty days.

6. When I as a retreatant am involved with the exercises of the First Week, I should not try to escape from total attention upon those considerations by looking to the areas of the later Weeks. At each stage of the retreat, I should work as if my whole response to God is found in the matter at hand. [11]

7. In making the Exercises I should ordinarily spend one full hour for each formal prayer period suggested by the director. When I feel tempted to cut short the hour, I should recognize the temptation for what it is—the first steps of taking back from God my total gift—and extend the time of prayer for a few minutes beyond the set time. [12]

8. When I find prayer a joy, I may well be tempted so to prolong the period of prayer that soon I find myself responding to the consolations of God more than to God himself. At such times, the observance of the set hour is a safeguard against subtle self-seeking even in prayer. When I find prayer dry and even a burden, I must be sure to spend the full hour as part of my attempt to respond by waiting for the Lord. [13]

9. If I feel a disorder in my attachment to a person, to a job or position, to a certain dwelling place, a certain city, country, and so on, I should take it to the Lord and pray insistently to be given the grace to free myself from such disorder. What I want above all is the ability to respond freely to God, and all other loves for people, places, and things are held in proper perspective by the light and strength of God's grace. [16]

10. I should be aware that the director, even if a priest, is not necessarily my confessor. It is not essential for the director to know my past sins or even my present state of sin. At the same time, however, the attempt to speak out my temptations and fears, the consolations and lights given me by God, the various movements that happen within me, is the great advantage of a directed retreat, wherein the director can listen, sometimes enlighten, and adapt the progress of the retreat according to the way I am being led by God and responding to him. Without this openness between myself as a retreatant and the director, the retreat itself will not be able to be adapted and focused so as to lead to the growth which is possible for me. [17]

B. *For the Director*

[2]   1. The director's role is that of helper. I help by explaining the different ways of praying. I help by suggesting the matter to be considered in prayer, and I do not hinder God's movements in the retreatant by imposing my own interpretations of Scripture or of theology. The Exercises are, above all, a time for intimate contact between God and the retreatant, and the retreatant will profit far more from the understanding and love aroused by the grace of God than from the rhetoric or brilliance of me as the retreat director.

[6]   2. I should expect that in the course of a Week the retreatant will be moved in various ways. When the retreatant claims that nothing is happening in prayer, I should ask how the retreatant goes about his prayer, at what times he prays, where he prays, and in general how he spends the day. Sometimes what appears to be an action or event of small consequences can affect the course of prayer for a whole day or a number of days. This again is an area where I as a director can be a great help by the kind of questioning which may uncover the cause that blocks the openness to God's call.

[7]   3. When the retreatant is in a time of temptation or desolation, I should be a kind listener and gentle support. To the best of my ability, I should help to expose the ways in which the powers of evil attempt to block the retreatant's ability to respond to God. I should remind the retreatant that God continues to be at hand even at such times with the necessary grace of strength and light.

[8]   4. As the retreatant begins to be aware of the various movements in himself, whether of consolation or desolation, I should determine when it would be helpful to explain further the ways for discerning the sources of such movement so that the retreatant is better able to understand how to respond to God.

[9]   5. Since there are different sets of instructions about the way we are moved in the First Week in distinction to the Second Week and thereafter, I should be careful to present and explain only what is more immediately helpful to the retreatant for where he is at present in his retreat. Otherwise, confusion can result from the very explanations which were meant to be a help.

6. In the First Week, it often happens that the retreatant will [10] be tempted to discouragement or rejection by thoughts about his own unworthiness before God, the costs of such a loving response, or fear for what others might think or say of him. I will find the Guidelines for the Discernment of Spirits for the First Week, in [314-327] below on pages 75-79, helpful to present at this time. By contrast, in the Second Week, the temptation which the retreatant often faces comes more from the appeal and attraction of some good, real or apparent. At this time, I will find the Guidelines for the Discernment of Spirits for the Second Week, in [328-336] below, more helpful.

7. I should be cautious when a retreatant is uplifted by con- [14] solation or fervor so that he desires to make great plans or to pronounce some sort of vow. While I as the director should respect idealism, I must be able to weigh the gifts of God, along with the natural endowments of personality, character, and intelligence, as I work with the retreatant.

8. I must always provide the balance for a retreatant, both in [15] times of exhilaration and in times of discouragement. I myself am not the one who should urge a particular decision—for example, to enter religious life, to marry this or that person, or to take a vow of poverty. My effort as director is always to facilitate the movement of God's grace within the retreatant so that the light and love of God inflame all possible decisions and resolutions about life situations. I should always remember that God is not only Creator but truly *the* Director of this person's retreat; I myself should never provide a hindrance to such an intimate communication.

9. It is my role as a director to adapt the Spiritual Exercises [18] to each retreatant, in view of his age and maturity, his education, and also his potential and his talents. I should decide what exercises would prove useless or even harmful to a retreatant because of a lack of physical strength or natural ability as well as what exercises would benefit and perhaps challenge a retreatant who is properly disposed and endowed. I may often discover that a retreatant at this particular time of life has neither the ability nor sometimes the desire to go beyond what is ordinarily described as the exercises of the First Week. So, too, I should make the judgment whether the full Exercises would be profitable to a particular retreatant at this time. Because the

Exercises are a limited instrument through which God can work, I should be aware that many persons would not be able to enter well into the Exercises, perhaps because of a lack of natural talents, perhaps because of a certain kind of personality, or perhaps because God does not draw them to respond through the structured method of these Exercises.

[19]   10. I may want to help a retreatant of talent and proper disposition through the full Exercises, but carried on in the face of normal occupations and living conditions for the extent of the whole retreat. As director I should determine, along with the retreatant, the amount of time possible each day for prayer and divide up the matter accordingly. If an hour and a half can be secured daily by the retreatant, the retreat could progress slowly, with almost a single point providing enough material for such a length of prayer. For example, in the First Exercise of the First Week, each single example of sin might provide the matter to be considered in prayer for that day. So, too, in the mysteries of Our Lord's life, I may find it helpful to have the retreatant return to the same mystery for three or four days in succession.

SPIRITUAL EXERCISES [21]

The structure of these exercises has the purpose of leading a person to a true spiritual freedom. We attain this goal by gradually bringing an order of values into our lives so that we make no choice or decisions because we have been influenced by some disordered attachment or love.

PRESUPPOSITION [22]

For a good relationship to develop between the retreatant and the director and for the continual progress of the retreat, a mutual respect is very necessary. This may be especially true in areas of scriptural and theological presentation. A favorable interpretation by the director or by the retreatant should always be given to the other's statement. If misinterpretation seems possible, it should be cleared up with Christian understanding. So, too, if actual error seems to be held, the best possible interpretation should be presented so that a more correct understanding might develop.

[THE FIRST WEEK]

[23]

THE FOUNDATION: FACT AND PRACTICE

God freely created us so that we might know, love, and serve him in this life and be happy with him forever. God's purpose in creating us is to draw forth from us a response of love and service here on earth, so that we may attain our goal of everlasting happiness with him in heaven.

All the things in this world are gifts of God, created for us, to be the means by which we can come to know him better, love him more surely, and serve him more faithfully.

As a result, we ought to appreciate and use these gifts of God insofar as they help us toward our goal of loving service and union with God. But insofar as any created things hinder our progress toward our goal, we ought to let them go.

In everyday life, then, we should keep ourselves indifferent or undecided in the face of all created gifts when we have an option and we do not have the clarity of what would be a better choice. We ought not to be led on by our natural likes and dislikes even in matters such as health or sickness, wealth or poverty, between living in the east or in the west, becoming an accountant or a lawyer.

Rather, our only desire and our one choice should be that option which better leads us to the goal for which God created us.

Note: This consideration is to be read over by the retreatant a few times each day during the first few days of the retreat. As is evident, these words express the basic Christian catechesis in the general terms of salvation. The prayer of the retreatant at this time may well be guided by scriptural texts which will enlighten and reinforce the notions contained in this foundation (see the suggested SCRIPTURE TEXTS, A, numbers 1-13, at [261], pages 64-66 below).

First Exercise [45]

PREPARATION: I always take a moment to call to mind the [46] attitude of reverence with which I approach this privileged time with God. I re-collect everything up to this moment of my day— my thoughts and words, what I have done and what has happened to me—and ask that God direct it all to his praise and to his service.

Note: This preparatory prayer, marking the beginning of each formal prayer period, not only reinforces the continuing petition for God's gift of reverence in me but also calls to mind how I must continue to beg that my total day is by his grace more and more integrated and centered in him alone.

GRACE: There is an importance in my speaking out the area [48] of my need for God's grace according to the time, subject matter, and my own dispositions during the retreat. Perhaps it may also act as a preparation of my inner being for an openness to God's entrance into a particular area of my life.

In this First Exercise, the grace I seek is the gift of feeling [47] shame and confusion before God as I consider the effects of even one sin as compared with my own sinful life. I may find it helpful to imagine myself as bound, helpless, alienated as I enter into these exercises dealing with sin.

THE SETTING: (1) the angels who rebelled against God. [50]

It has been a deep part of our Christian heritage to understand that the first rejection of God's love in his creation is found among his special messengers, the angels. Theologically and spiritually, the sin of the angels exemplified the radical choice of self before God, which is the essence of sin, and the terrifying but necessary consequence of rejecting the very source of all our life and love. Pure spirits of decisive knowledge and totalizing love, the angels somehow were presented with the choice which God continues to give to each person he has lovingly made— whether we freely choose to respond to the life and love which he offers to us. Some angels chose to reject his free offer of love and life with him forever. Immediately by closing themselves off from God, they changed from a life of grace to a death-hatred of God and found themselves in their own choice of hell.

I mull over this sin in my mind, letting its decisiveness strike deep into my heart, and then I look to my many rejections of God's love.

[51]   THE SETTING: (2) the sin of Adam and Eve.

In the Biblical account of how sin entered into our world from the time of the first man, we once again get a picture of a very simple but direct rejection of God's love. Adam and Eve want to be as God is, and so they are described as eating the forbidden fruit of the tree of knowledge. Both try to escape the responsibility of the choice which each one has made by trying to shift the blame to someone or something else. The effect of this one sin is not only the loss of God's special sharing of his life in grace for all mankind, but also the continuing flow of evil perpetrated by men upon their fellowmen and their world.

I consider the effect of this first sin of man and woman for themselves and for all their posterity. I let the destructiveness of evil become fully present to my attention. If one sin can wreak such havoc, what about my own sinfulness?

[52]   THE SETTING: (3) the person who goes to hell.

There is the possibility of a person making a definitive "no" as a response to God's love and ratifying that "no" even in death. By the "no" one has given to God, one has chosen self and therefore all the opposite of the love and life forces which can have their source only in God. One has condemned oneself to the death of hell for all eternity.

How can I measure the number of "no's" which I have spoken to God up to this time? What can I say to God about myself?

[53]   COLLOQUY: I put myself before Jesus Christ our Lord, present before me on the cross. I talk to him about how he creates because he loves and then he becomes man out of love, so emptying himself as to pass from eternal life to death here in time, even death on a cross, that by his obedience of love given to his Father he might die for my sins.

I look to myself and ask—just letting the question penetrate my being:

In the past, what response have I made to Christ?

How do I respond to Christ now?

What response should I make to Christ? As I look upon Jesus as he hangs upon the cross, I ponder whatever God may bring to my attention.

I close with an Our Father.

[55]   Second Exercise

> PREPARATION: I always come to prayer, conscious of the reverence I owe to my God. I beg that everything of my day He may direct more and more to his praise and service.
>
> GRACE: In this Second Exercise, I ask God for the gift of a growing and intense sorrow, even to the depth of tears if it be his grace, for all my sins.

[56]   THE SETTING: I see myself as a sinner—bound, helpless, alien-ated—before a loving God and all his gifts of creation.

[57]   Without the detail of an examination of conscience, I let pass before my mind all my sins and sinful tendencies that permeate my life from my youth up to the very present moment. I let the weight of such evil, all stemming from me, be felt throughout my whole being.

[58]   To gain even greater perspective on my sin, I reflect that out of me—one human person among the millions of men who live—so much evil, hatred, and death can come forth. What can I compare myself to—a sewer polluting the waters of the river of life? a walking contagion of diseases who continues to walk throughout my world, affecting it and my fellowmen without warning?

I feel the weight and horror of so many effects of my sinful acts.

[59]   I put myself before God, and look at the contrast: God, the source of life, and I, a cause of death; God, the source of love, and I, with all my petty jealousies and hatreds; God, from whom all good gifts come, and I, with my attempts to win favor, buy attention, be well thought of, and so on.

[60]   I look at my world. Everything cooperates to continue to give me life and strength. I look at the whole support system of air, warmth, light and darkness, products of the earth, works of men's hands—everything contributes to my well-being.

I think of the people who have prayed for me and love me.

The whole communion of saints has interest in my salvation and actively works to try to help me.

Everywhere I look, the more astonished I become, seeing so much good coming in on me, while I issue forth so many evils.

COLLOQUY: How can I respond to a God so good to me in [61] himself and surrounding me with the goodness of his holy ones and all the gifts of his creation? All I can do is give thanks, wondering at his forgiving love, which continues to give me life up to this very moment. By his grace, I want to amend.

I close with an Our Father.

Third Exercise [62]

PREPARATION: There is the usual prayerful reverence and dedication of my day, consciously recalled as I enter into this formal prayer period.

GRACE: As in the Second Exercise, I continue to beg our Lord for the gift of a growing and intense sorrow, even to the depth of tears if it be his grace, for all my sins.

THE SETTING: Rather than take up new subject matter for consideration, I should return to those thoughts and feelings which struck me forcefully from the First and Second Exercises. I review those areas in which I felt greater consolation or desolation or, in general, greater spiritual appreciation. The idea of the repetition is to let sink further into my heart the movements of God through the means of subject matter already presented.

In the midst of these considerations, a threefold colloquy is suggested, to show the intensity of my desire for God's gift of sorrow.

COLLOQUY:

[63]   (a) First I go to Mary, our Mother, that she may ask, on my behalf, grace for three favors from her Son and Lord:

1. A deep realization of what sin in my life is, and a feeling of abhorrence at my own sinful acts;
2. Some understanding of the disorder in my life due to sin and sinful tendencies, that I may begin to know how to amend my life and bring order into it;
3. An insight into the world that stands opposed to Christ, that I may put off from myself all that is worldly and vain.

Then I say a Hail Mary or a Memorare, or the like.

(b) Next in the company of Mary, I ask the same petitions of her Son, that Jesus may obtain these graces from the Father for me. Then I say the "Soul of Christ" or some such prayer to Jesus.

(c) Finally I approach the Father, having been presented by both Jesus and Mary. Again I make the same requests of the Father, that he, the giver of all good gifts, may grant them to me.

Then I close with an Our Father.

[64]
Fourth Exercise

This period of prayer is meant to be a repetition again— sometimes called a summary or a résumé. The hope is that the mind becomes less and less active with ideas since the subject matter does not change, and as a result the heart is more and more central to the way I find myself responding. The prayer period itself will probably be less active on one hand, and yet on the other by the grace of God it will grow in intensity. The intensity of the prayer is concretized by praying once again in the manner of the threefold colloquy.

[65]
Fifth Exercise

PREPARATION: The usual prayerful reverence and dedication of my day is recalled.

GRACE: I beg for a deep sense of the pain of loss which envelops the damned, so that if I were ever to lose sight of the loving goodness of God, at least the fear of such a condemnation will keep me from falling into sin.

THE SETTING: an experience of hell. [66,
67,
St. Paul speaks of our being able to grasp the breadth and 68,
length and height and depth of Christ's love and experiencing
this love which surpasses all knowledge (Eph. 3:18-19). At 69,
its opposite pole, I try to experience the breadth and length 70]
and height and depth of hell—the despair of facing a cross
with no one on it, the turning out upon a world which has
no God, the total emptiness of living, an environment pervasive with hatred and self-seeking, a living death.

I bring the whole of my being into the vividness of this experience. I let all the horror of sin which has been the fruit of my previous prayer periods wash over me in an immersing flood. In many ways, this setting is the most passive of prayer experiences; it is not a matter of thinking new thoughts or even of looking for new images, but rather building on the whole experience of sin in which I have immersed myself in the past prayer periods. It is akin to the passive way my senses take in sights, smells, sounds, feelings, as an automatic datum for my attention. I know that the total felt-environment of sin, in whatever ways it can be most vividly mine, is the setting for this period of prayer.

COLLOQUY: Once I have let the awfulness of this experience [71]
sink deep within me, I begin to talk to Christ our Lord about
it. I talk to him about all the people who have lived—the many
who lived before his coming and who deliberately closed in
upon themselves and chose such a hell for all eternity, the
many who walked with him in his own country and who rejected his call to love, the many who still keep rejecting the
call to love and remain locked in their own chosen hell.

I give thanks to Jesus that he has not put an end to my life and allowed me to fall into any of these groups. All I can do is give thanks to him that up to this very moment he has shown himself so loving and merciful to me. Then I close with an Our Father.

[72]   **HELPS TO PROCEEDING IN THE FIRST WEEK**

The model of exercises presented here indicates the way of proceeding in the First Week. The usual prayer pattern consists of five formal prayer periods of one hour each. Two presentations of matter are given—in the First and Second Exercises. The remaining three periods of prayer are meant to be less demanding of thought, simpler and quieter, and a deepening of what has moved me. The last or fifth period of prayer (traditionally called an Application of Senses) is meant to be least cognitive; it is an attempt to let all that has been my experience in the previous prayer periods to pour over me once again in one summarizing and totalizing experience, out of which I can once again speak to my God.

A typical day of the First Week could use the Five Exercises just as they are. Each day of the Week could continue to be a repetition of these exact same exercises. There is also the possibility of using various scripture texts to let God's word enlighten the experience indicated in the exercises. In this way, scripture texts may so be chosen that the experience of just the First or Second Exercise may permeate the entire day for two or three days apiece.

In any case, the pattern of the day as well as of the Week is meant to be clear. Each day should begin with no more than two presentations of scriptural matter, with the succeeding repetitions allowing the prayer to grow simpler, quieter, and more affective. So, too, the First Week is seen as a progression from days of more active thought and turmoil of feeling to its closing days of deep sorrow, acceptance, and thanks to God my Savior. The First Week suggests all that is integral to the basic Christian conversion experience: "Repent and believe the good news."

There is also the possibility of including other matters for consideration in this First Week when it is judged that it will be helpful for a particular retreatant. Matter on death itself or judgment might be presented in a manner similar to the exercises indicated in the First Week or else in a scriptural way. The only norm for the presentation of further ideas is the good progress of the retreatant.

Although five exercises are suggested for the duration of the First Week, age, condition of health, and the physical constitution of the exercitant may indicate that four exercises or less may be more profitable. When five exercises are used, the retreat day is ordinarily patterned to begin with the first period of prayer at midnight. "Midnight" does not describe actual time, but rather indicates that the prayer period should be set after an initial experience of deep sleep, which for many people comes within some two to three hours of sleeping time. It is at this time when both body and mind are relaxed and quiet that the prayer period can be very fruitful. The other four periods of prayer can easily be spaced throughout the day.

Aids for Prayer   [73-

The purpose of these directions is to help us to be better   90]
disposed as we move into the formal prayer periods and so
to be more open to the movements of God within us.

A. *Recollection*

My whole day should be consistent with my prayer. There   [73]
are particular moments within the day that can be capitalized
on to help bring this about:

1. As I go to bed, I briefly recall the area about which my
prayer will center on the following day. I ask God's blessings
on my efforts this coming day.

2. When I wake up, I should not let my thoughts roam at   [74]
random, but once again I recall the direction of this whole
day's prayer and ask for God's continual help. Insofar as I am
able, I will find it an aid to keep myself in this recollected
mood all the while I dress.

3. As it has been noted in the description of the First Exer- [75]
cise and thereafter, a conscious recall of what I am about and
whose presence I am in is most helpful at the beginning of
each formal prayer period. This should be done very briefly,
just to establish the sense of reverence and dedication which
should pervade my prayer time.

4. In a similar way, every prayer period is centered in what   [54]
has been called a colloquy. *Colloquy* is a term that describes
the intimate conversation between the Father and me, Christ
and me, Mary or one of the saints and me, and so on. This
conversation happens on the occasion of my putting myself
as totally as I can into the setting of the prayer; I will find

that I speak or listen as God's Spirit moves me—sometimes as sinner, sometimes as child, at other times as lover or friend, and so on. A colloquy does not take place at any particular time within the period of prayer; it takes place as I respond within the setting of the exercise. It is true that I should mark the actual end of the hour of prayer with a definite closure—usually the Our Father or some such common prayer is a reverent way of signifying the end of this formal prayer period.

B. *Position*

[76]   1. Formal prayer can be made in almost any bodily position. Certain positions are more helpful for some people than for others, just as certain positions are more helpful at one time in prayer than at another. The important aspect of position is found in the criteria whether I can be at ease and yet attentive, reverent yet relaxed. And so kneeling, sitting, standing, prostrate are all potential positions for prayer. Walking, too, may lend itself to praying well if it can image the relaxation and reflectivity of the exercise. But walking often can become a restless pacing back and forth which may have its effect upon the restlessness of the prayer of my inner being.

The only restriction upon positions in prayer arises from my awareness that a certain position may be a distraction for others, for example, to lie prostrate in a church or public chapel, where my position would call attention to myself and hence should not be used.

2. Once I have adopted a position in prayer and my prayer is going well, I should not readily change position because again the outward restlessness or shifting of position can jar the inner calm of prayer. Often a certain rhythm of kneeling and sitting, standing or walking, is helpful according to the moods of reflection and intense begging within the exercise.

C. *Review*

[77]   1. After a formal prayer period is finished, I should review what happened during the past hour—not so much what ideas did I have, but more the movements of consolation, desolation, fear, anxiety, boredom, and so on, and perhaps something about my distractions, especially if they were deep or disturbing. I thank God for his favors and ask pardon for my own negligences of the prayer time. Often it is good to signalize

the difference of this review of prayer from the prayer period itself by some change of place or position.

2. I should spend about fifteen minutes in such a review. I may find it very helpful to jot down the various reflections that strike me so that I can more easily discuss with my director what has been my progress from prayer period to prayer period of this past day.

D. *Environment*

My whole surrounding, as well as my own deportment, can contribute to the prayerful atmosphere of the retreat or detract from it. Some areas which I could pay special attention to are:

1. During the exercises of the First Week, I may find it con- [79] ducive to a deeper entrance into the mystery of sin and evil by setting my prayer periods in places which are dark and deprived of light—keeping my own room dark, taking advantage of the dimness of a chapel or church, and so on. In general, I restrict my movements during this week, avoiding the pleasantness of sun and beauties of nature, the better to focus my attention on the darkness and loathsomeness of sin.

I continue to adapt such directions as these to fit the particular mood of the prayer of the Week in which I am currently involved.

2. In regard to myself during the First Week, it is important [78] that I keep my attention on the matter at hand, and do not subtly seek for ways to escape and relieve the awfulness of sin which may be building up within me. I do not dwell on things which would give me joy and pleasure—whether friends, occupations, music, food, or anything else. Rather I keep my thoughts more focused on the serious side of life.

For the same reason, I do not try to find occasions to laugh, [80] knowing how often laughter can be the attempt to escape the uneasiness of a situation. So, too, I must be more conscious of not trying to look around for distractions; it is helpful to keep a certain modesty of the eyes—always with the intention [81] of aiding the singleness of focus within my whole prayer environment.

[82]   E. *Penance*

1. General Description

Penance must always be seen in terms of my love response to God. Penance can be divided into two kinds: interior and exterior penance. The more important is interior penance; it is the grace which is sought throughout the First Week and can be described as a deep sorrow for one's sins and a firm purpose of amendment, especially in terms of an ever more full-hearted response of love in God's service. Confession received its formal name of the sacrament of penance (now called the sacrament of reconciliation) because of these interior sentiments of the sacramental encounter.

Exterior penance properly flows out of the grace of interior penance. It consists in taking on a certain self-inflicted punishment, either through denying ourselves something or through some positive action, to concretize our regret and resolution about our failings in our love response to God and neighbor. There are times, however, when exterior penance does not flow out of grace already received, but rather I take on this kind of penance to signalize further my effort and prayer in begging God for the gift of interior penance. In this latter case, I must be very diligent in following the advice of my director. The reason why advice is important is that more penance is better for some, and less for others. When I am seeking a particular grace and I seem not to find it, it may be the time for working out with the director some alternating periods of days in which I practice some penance and days in which I do not. The counsel of the director is very important at this time since I can easily be taken in by the subtle deception of thinking I can force God's hand by my penance or, more generally, that I am the one who can bring about such a gift because of my penance. Another reason that the director should always be kept informed lies in the area of my own self-deception: (a) either I am too ready to try to escape from any penance by using all kinds of subterfuges, such as "it is medieval," "I am not strong enough," "it's not for me," and so on; (b) or I am not properly ordered in my use of penance so that I attempt too much fasting, or too many vigils, or try to take on certain discomforts with the result that my prayer begins to suffer or I so weaken myself in this way very gradually that I am not able to sustain the retreat. Working with my director, I may be granted the grace by God our Lord, who knows our nature far better than we do, to understand what penance is suitable for me and when are the more suitable times for doing some penance.

Ordinarily, just as in the positions of prayer, I do not make a change in doing or not doing penance if God's grace continues to be operative in leading me ever deeper into the exercises of the retreat. So, too, at certain times during the retreat, penance seems to be called for whereas at other times penance would add a jarring note to my prayer. In every case, the counsel of the director is most important.

2. Purpose of Exterior Penance

Three principal purposes for performing some exterior penance at certain times are:

(a) Traditionally described, penance makes satisfaction for [87] past sins. Knowing that we truly are body-persons, we have the experience of "the spirit is willing, but the flesh is weak." This is oftentimes true because of the very areas of sinfulness in our past. The taking on of a bodily penance is an attempt to bring about that oneness of my inner and outer being to go specifically against the traces and scars which sin has left in me.

(b) In a similar way, I take on exterior penance as a con- [88] crete reminder to myself that I do have to exercise a control, especially as I perform penances that touch those areas of my life where little or no control has been shown in the past. By the grace of God, this example of control through the exercise of penance shows forth the growth of my own human freedom.

(c) More directly relevant to the retreat, perhaps, I per- [89] form some exterior penance because of some grace or gift I desire very earnestly, and I want to involve the wholeness of my being in this request before God. Often when such grace is granted, for example, the gift of deep sorrow for one's sins in the First Week or the gift of anguish with Christ in anguish in the Third Week, I may then feel moved to do some penance to enter more fully into the mysteries about which I am praying.

3. Kinds of Exterior Penance

Three principal ways of performing some exterior penance are:

(a) Eating: If we do away with what is superfluous, it is [83] not penance, but temperance. We do penance when we deny ourselves something of what is proper and good for us. We should never do away with what is necessary for us since then we would be destroying the very purpose of our taking on penance—that we might better respond to God in the prayer exercises of the retreat. If any physical harm or illness results from penance in this area, we should be aware that it is not suitable penance for us.

[84]   (b) Sleep: If we do away with the superfluous in what is pampering and soft, it is not penance. We do penance when we take something away in our manner of sleeping that is proper and good for us. Once again if we find ourselves too sleepy to pray or eventual illness results, we know that we have over-stepped the bounds of suitable penance. People truly differ in their sleep needs, and we should always try to get enough that will enable us to work full-heartedly in God's service.

[85]   (c) Bodily penances: There has been a tradition among many religious groups to have commonly recognized bodily penances, such as the wearing of a hairshirt, the taking of a discipline or whipping oneself with light cords, and the wearing of some kind of blunt-pointed chain around the waist or arm or leg. These kinds of penances coming down through our Christian tradition still may point the way to profitable forms of bodily penance today.

[86]   It should be obvious that bodily penances are not meant to cause wounds, sickness, and so on, but rather they are aimed at willingly sought-out pain or discomfort because I am moti-vated by love. The possible areas of taking on discomfort or seeking out inconveniences for penance are very numerous, and those are chosen as most suitable and safe forms of penance which we find make us more aware of our attempts to express our love for God and for our fellowmen.

[24, 25, 26, 90]   F. *The Examination of Conscience and Confession*

1. Although the retreat is already an inwardly reflective time, it is often found helpful to set aside a brief time about mid-way in the day and again at the end of the day before retiring in a formal review of how I have spent the day. Within the retreat, this examination of conscience is not so much aimed at reviewing the areas of sinfulness, but rather at the fulfillment of all those aids of position, recollection, environment, and so on, which are meant to integrate my day, more wholly fixing it on God. Since the Weeks as well as individual days within the

Week may make very different demands for such an integration, I will find this style of particular examination especially helpful in maintaining the proper spirit.

2. Some retreatants find that it is very useful to keep some sort of record of this particular examination both to compare the noon and evening periods as well as the progress from day to day within the Week. Others may find a written record too mechanical and do not profit from it. The better progress of the retreat is always the norm for use or non-use of a particular method. [27, 28, 29, 30, 31]

3. The format of the particular examination can be the same as that style of prayer used for making a general examination of conscience, whether practiced daily or at the time of confession. There are five points in this method of approach: [32]

[43]

(a) giving thanks to God our Lord for all the favors he has given;

(b) asking the help of the Spirit to enlighten me so that I may see my sin as he sees it;

(c) going back over the events of the day or of the time since my last confession to see the sinful acts, whether in thoughts, words, or deeds, whether of omission or commission, and the tendencies or roots of such sinful behavior;

(d) expressing my sorrow and asking God's forgiving love to heal me;

(e) praying for the strength of God's grace to help me amend my life.

4. There usually develops a desire for the sacrament of penance as we enter deeply into the exercises of the First Week. Not only should confession be encouraged, but it is well to consider the advantages of a general confession at this time: [44]

(a) While there is no obligation to make a general confession, at a time when I have let the full burden of my sinfulness weigh me down, I come with even greater sorrow to present to the Lord all the sin and perversities which are so deeply a part of my person.

(b) Through means of prayer, I arrive at a far deeper insight into my sins and their malice. Because the grace of the retreat has led me to this deeper knowledge and sorrow, I come with greater fervor and openness to the healing power of Christ in the sacrament of penance.

(c) It is good to make such a confession, whether it be a general confession or not, somewhere towards the end of the

First Week so that I approach the sacrament not in haste or turmoil over the recognition of my sins, but rather in accepting myself as sinner, as one always in need of radical healing, and as one who acknowledges that God alone is my Savior.

THE SECOND WEEK

CHRIST THE KING AND HIS CALL [91]

PREPARATION: I take the usual time to place myself before God in reverence and to beg him to direct everything in my day more and more to his service and praise.

GRACE: I ask of our Lord that I might be able to hear his call, and that I might be ready and willing to do what he wants.

THE SETTING: There are two unequal parts in this consideration, the first one naturally leading to the more important second part.

1. In the first part, let me put myself into a mythical situation—the kind of story-truth of which fairy tales are made. I imagine a human leader, selected and raised up by God our Lord himself; every man, woman, and child of good will is drawn to listen to such a leader and is inspired to follow his call. [92]

His address to all men rings out in words like these: "I want to overcome all diseases, all poverty, all ignorance, all oppression and slavery—in short, all the enemies of mankind. Whoever wishes to join me in this undertaking must be content with the same food, drink, clothing, and so on, as mine. So, too, he must work with me by day, and watch with me by night, that as he has had a share in the toil with me, afterwards he may share in the victory with me." If a leader so attractive and inspiring and so much a man of God makes such a call, what kind of a person could refuse such an invitation? How could anyone not want to be a part of so challenging and noble an adventure? [93]

[95]   2. In the second part, I consider Jesus Christ our Lord and his call. If a human leader can have such an appeal to us, how much greater is the attraction of the God-Man, Jesus Christ, our Leader and King! His call goes out to the whole of mankind, yet he specially calls each person in a particular way. He makes the appeal: "It is my will to win over the whole world, to conquer sin, hatred, and death—all the enemies between mankind and God. Whoever wishes to join me in this mission must be willing to labor with me, so that by following me in suffering, he may follow me in glory."

[96]   With God inviting and with victory assured, how can anyone of right mind not give himself over to Jesus and his work?

[97]   Persons who are of great heart and are set on fire with zeal to follow Jesus Christ, eternal King and Lord of all, will not only offer themselves entirely for such a mission, but will act against anything that would make their response less total. They would want to express themselves in some such words as these:

[98]   "Eternal Lord and King of all creation, humbly I come before you. Knowing the support of Mary, your mother, and all your saints, I am moved by your grace to offer myself to you and to your work. I deeply desire to be with you in accepting all wrongs and all abuse and all poverty, both actual and spiritual —and I deliberately choose this, if it is for your greater service and praise. If you, my Lord and King, would so call and choose me, then take and receive me into such a way of life."

SUGGESTED DIRECTIONS

[99]   1. The above exercise should be considered in formal prayer twice during the day. The rest of the day is free of set prayer periods.

[100]   2. During the Second Week and thereafter, it can be profitable to read some classic spiritual works or some biographies of holy men and women. Scripture, too, can sometimes be used, although it is not wise to read the Gospels since certain mysteries of our Lord's life and ministry may call forth responses from me that are not consonant with where I am in my formal prayer periods of the retreat. The director and the retreatant should work out this area of reading together so that no influences contrary to the movement of the retreat are unwittingly introduced through the reading material.

The Incarnation

PREPARATION: I take the usual time to place myself before God in reverence and beg that he direct everything in my day more and more to his praise and service.

GRACE: I ask for the grace to know Jesus intimately, to love [104] him more intensely, and so to follow him more closely.

Preliminary Note: The following description is an attempt to point out some of the ways of entering into the style of prayer called "contemplation." The description in words can make it sound very mechanical. To remember that the act of praying is our single focus will pour life-blood into the dead body of words. [102, 103, 106, 107, 108]

THE SETTING: I try to enter into the vision of God, in his triune life, looking upon our world: men and women aimless, despairing, hateful and killing, men and women sick and dying, the old and the young ,the rich and the poor, the happy and the sad, some being born and some being laid to rest. The leap of divine joy: God knows that the time has come when the mystery of his salvific plan, hidden from the beginning of the world, will become manifest.

This is the context of the Annunciation scene, which we find in the text of Scripture (Luke 1:26-38). I try to stay with the eyes of God, and look upon the young girl Mary, as she is greeted by Gabriel.

I let myself be totally present to the scene, hearing the nuances of the questions, seeing the expression in the face and eyes, watching the gestures and movements which tell us so much about a person.

I notice how our triune God works—so simply and quietly. A world goes on, apparently oblivious of the total revolution which has begun. I look at Mary's complete way of responding to her Lord and God.

COLLOQUY: As I find myself immersed in the setting of this [109] mystery of the Incarnation, I may want just to stay with Mary or with our Lord, who has now become man for me. Sometimes

I may want to speak out my joy, my thanks, my wonder, or my praise. According to the light I have received, I beg for the grace to know and to be able to draw close to Jesus, my Lord. I close the prayer period with an Our Father.

[110]   **The Second Contemplation**

                         The Nativity

PREPARATION: I take the usual time to place myself before God in reverence and beg that he direct everything in my day more and more to his praise and service.

[113]   GRACE: I continue to ask for the grace to know Jesus intimately, to be able to love him more intensely, and so to follow him more closely.

[111,   THE SETTING: The familiar story of the Nativity should allow me the more easily to be present fully to the persons and places
112,   of this mystery. Whatever methods help me enter into the whole
114,   scene and to be with the persons involved I should embrace.

115,
116]   To be able to enter into the deep-down stillness of this night, to be able to see this very human baby with all the wonder which comes from eyes of faith, to watch how Mary and Joseph handle themselves, their own response to God at this time—these are various aspects or focuses of the mystery to which I may find myself drawn.

        I should take note of the hardship which is already so much a part of Jesus' presence in our world. The labors of the journey to Bethlehem, the struggles of finding a shelter, the poverty, hunger, thirst, heat, and cold, the insults which meet the arrival of God-with-us—all this that he might die on the cross for me.

[117]   COLLOQUY: According to the different aspects which I may focus upon at any one time within the prayer period, I respond accordingly, for example, to Mary, Joseph, Jesus, the Father. Perhaps there is little to say because this style of contemplation is often more a "being with" experience than a word-response.

        I always bring the period of prayer to a close with an Our Father.

The Third Contemplation [118]

A Repetition

This period is a repetition of the First and Second Exercises. After the preparatory reverence and dedication of my day, and the petition for grace, the matter from the First or Second Exercises, or from both together, is used. Quite often I find that I would like to return to a particular mystery in itself, such as the Incarnation; or I might find that in this Third Contemplation, the original first two settings flow one into the other. In making such a repetition, it is always important to return to those parts or points of focus where I have experienced understanding, consolation, or desolation.

Since the entrance into the setting of such a repetition is frequently very simple, the emphasis more and more is fixed on my personal response which is represented by the colloquy. I should always remember to close the prayer period with an Our Father.

In this repetition and in all those which follow, the usual [119] manner of proceeding is observed as it was explained in the First Week. The subject matter is changed, but the same manner of repeating the exercise is continued.

The Fourth Contemplation [120]

A Résumé

This period reinforces the notion of the repetition as outlined in the preceding paragraph. I might note how the prayer usually grows simpler in the matter considered, allowing always for a deeper and deeper personal response to the mysteries of Christ's life.

The Fifth Contemplation [121]

Application of Senses

Traditionally this prayer period has been described as an application of the five senses to the matter of the day.

[122, 123, 124, 125]   After the preparatory prayer and the petition for the usual grace, this last period of prayer within my day is meant to be my own "letting go," a total immersion of myself into the mystery of Christ's life this day. Just as when we tried to enter into the experience of hell within the First Week, so here too, it is not a matter of thinking new thoughts or of trying new methods of getting into the mystery. Rather the notion is to build upon all the experiences which have been a part of my prayer day. Again it is akin to the passive way my senses take in sights, smells, sounds, feelings, as an automatic datum for my attention. The total felt-environment of the particular mystery of Christ's life, in whatever ways it can be most vividly mine, is the setting for this final period of prayer in each day.

[126]   COLLOQUY: I respond as I am so moved by God's grace. I close with an Our Father.

FURTHER DIRECTIONS

1. It is important to point out that throughout this Week and [127] the subsequent Weeks, I read only the mystery which is the subject matter of my contemplation. I do not read any mystery which is not to be used on that particular day or at that hour, so that the contemplation of one mystery does not interfere with another.

2. An ideal suggested order of the prayer day is: The First [128] Exercise on the Incarnation should take place at midnight (that is, after an initial period of sleep), the second in early morning, the third in later morning, the fourth in the afternoon, and the fifth in the evening.

The order of the prayer day has its importance in terms of the whole ordering process of one's life, which is the end of the Exercises.

3. The Second Week may well call for some adaptation in the [129] number of prayer periods. Whether the person is old or young, weak or strong, quite often the First Week has been a tiring experience. For that reason, it is often better not to use the midnight meditation time, with the possibility of either five or four periods of prayer spread out throughout the day.

4. It is probably obvious that some adaptation should be made [130] in terms of the aids for prayer.

Specifically, as soon as I awake, I recall the direction of this whole day's prayer, with the desire to grow in my intimate knowledge of Jesus Christ in order to love and serve him better.

Another help will be to recall at various times in the day the mysteries of the life of Christ our Lord from his Incarnation up to the mystery I am currently contemplating.

So, too, I as a retreatant use darkness and light, the chapel or the outdoors, insofar as I understand that it fits well with the mystery I am contemplating.

In regard to penance, again I conduct myself according to the mysteries under consideration. Some may call for penance, others will not.

As a general reminder, I continue to observe very carefully all the aids for prayer which aim at the good progress of the retreat.

[131] 5. In a way of preparing myself similar to the preparation for the first prayer period of the day, I come to all periods of prayer in the following manner: as soon as I note that it is time for the next prayer period, even before moving on, I bring to mind where I am going, before whom I am to appear, and briefly recall the subject matter of the exercise. Then with a certain anticipation of God's gifts, I proceed to the usual preparatory reverence, as I enter into the very exercise itself.

[132]   **The Second Day**

On the second day, for the first and second contemplations, the Presentation in the Temple (see no. 35, at [268] below), and the Flight into Exile in Egypt (see no. 36, at [269] below), are used. Two repetitions, along with or including the Application of the Senses, are done as on the First Day.

[133] Note: As was stated previously, sometimes it will be profitable, no matter how strong and well-disposed the retreatant, to make some changes in the first part of this Second Week, in order to attain better what is desired. So the first contemplation would be the one on rising in the morning. Then there would be one later in the morning, with another in the afternoon, and the final one in the evening.

[134]   **The Third Day**

On the third day, I use the contemplations on the Obedience of the Child Jesus to his parents (see no. 38, at [271] below), and the Finding of the Child Jesus in the Temple (see no. 39, at [272] below). As usual there follow the two repetitions, along with or including the Application of the Senses.

INTRODUCTION TO THE CONSIDERATION [135]

OF

DIFFERENT STATES OF LIFE

One way of considering the mysteries of Jesus' early life is to see the interpretative direction in which they point. The ordinary life of the Christian is exemplified in Christ's obedience to his parents in the ordinary life of Nazareth. But the call to service in the Father's house is already manifested in the mystery of Jesus' remaining in the temple at the age of twelve to the consternation of his mother and father.

While I continue to contemplate his life, let me begin to examine myself and ask to what state of life or to what kind of life style is God in his loving providence leading me.

As a kind of introduction to this, in the next exercise, I consider the way Christ our Lord draws men and women, and on the other hand, the way the enemy of our human nature enslaves. At the same time I may also begin to see how I should prepare myself for a continued growth in whatever state or kind of life God our Lord may be moving me to choose.

The Fourth Day [136]

A Meditation on

TWO LEADERS, TWO STRATEGIES

We consider Christ, our Leader and Lord, our God and Brother, and we consider Satan, the personal enemy who sums up all the evils that beset mankind.

PREPARATION: I make the usual preparatory reverence and petition that God direct everything in my day more and more to his praise and service.

GRACE: I ask for the gift of being able to recognize the deceits [139] of Satan and for the help to guard myself against them; and also

33

I ask for a knowledge of the true life exemplified in Jesus Christ, my Lord and my God, and the grace to live my life in his way.

THE SETTING: There are two unequal parts in this considera-tion, the first one shedding light upon and giving direction to the more important second part.

[137,
138,
140,
141,
142]
1. To sum up all the forces of evil in the person of Satan makes me face the enormous power and oppression of evil itself. Keep-ing true to my own experience of the world, let me reflect how evil pummels the relations between nations and between peoples within a single country, so that no nation, no city, no state of life, no individual is left unscathed. I try to grasp the strategy of Satan as he attempts ever to enslave men and women and the world according to his design. People find themselves tempted to covet riches, and then because they possess some thing or things they find themselves seeking and accepting the honor and esteem of this world. From such honor arises the false sense of identity and value in which false pride has its roots.

So the strategy is simple: riches (or "this is mine") to honor (or "look at me") to pride (or "I AM . . ."). By these three steps, the evil one leads us to all other vices.

[143,
144,
145,
146]
2. Now let me look at Jesus Christ, who calls himself "the way, the truth, and the life." I notice how gently, but insistently, Jesus continues to call followers of all kinds and sends them forth to spread his good news to all people, no matter what their state or condition. Jesus adopts a strategy which is just the opposite of Satan: Try to help people, not enslave or oppress them. His method: Attract men and women to the highest spiri-tual poverty, and should it please God, and should he draw them to want to choose it, even to a life of actual poverty. Being poor, they will be led to accept and even to desire the insults and contempt of the world. The result will be a life of true humility.

Jesus' strategy is simple too: If I have been graced with the gift of poverty, then I am rich; if I have nothing, I have no power and I am despised and receive the contempt of the world; if I have nothing, my only possession is Christ and this is to be really true to myself—the humility of a person whose whole reality lies in being created and redeemed in Christ.

Through these three steps, Jesus and his apostles lead people to all other virtues.

COLLOQUY: Because of the importance of coming to some [147] understanding of the opposing forces of these two leaders and their strategies, I enter into the intensity of the prayer by addressing Mary, Christ, and the Father and begging favors from them.

(a) First I approach our Lady, asking her to obtain for me from her Son the grace-gift to be his apostle—following him in the highest spiritual poverty, and should God be pleased thereby and want to choose and accept me, even in actual poverty. Even greater is the gift I seek in being able to bear the insults and the contempt of my world, so imitating Christ my Lord ever more closely, provided only I can suffer these without sin on the part of another and without any offense to God. Then I say a Hail Mary or a Memorare.

(b) Next in the company of Mary, I ask the same petitions of her Son that Jesus may obtain these same favors or gifts from the Father. Then I say the "Soul of Christ" or some such prayer to Jesus.

(c) Finally I approach the Father, having been presented by both Jesus and Mary. Again, I make the same requests of the Father that he, the giver of all good gifts, may grant such favors to me. Then I close with an Our Father.

Note: This exercise is made three or four times within a single [148] day. The same three colloquies, with Our Lady, with her Son, and with the Father, close all the exercises as well as the one on the Three Types of Persons ([149-156] just below), which follows as the last (either fourth or fifth) prayer period of the day.

[149]   **THREE TYPES OF PERSONS**

> This is a meditation for the same fourth day to
> aid me in my freedom of choice according to
> God's call to me.

PREPARATION: I take the time for the usual preparatory
reverence and dedication of my day.

[152]   GRACE: I ask that I may be free enough to choose whatever
the lead of God's grace may indicate as his particular call to me.

[150,   THE SETTING: This prayer period is devoted to a consideration
151]   of three types of persons. Each one of them has taken in quite
a few possessions—not always with the best of motives, and in
fact sometimes quite selfishly. In general, each one is a good
person, and he would like to serve God, even to the extent that
if these possessions were to come in the way of his salvation,
he would like to be free of them.

[153]   1. The First Type—"a lot of talk, but no action"

This person keeps saying that he would like to stop being so
dependent on all the things which he possesses and which seem
to get in the way of his giving his life unreservedly to God. He
talks about the importance of saving his soul, but when death
comes, he is too busy about his possessions to have taken any
steps toward serving God.

[154]   2. The Second Type—"to do everything but the one thing
necessary"

This person would like to be free of all attachments which
get in the way of his relationship with God. But he would rather
work harder or fast or pray more—really just do about anything
but face the problem which he feels holds him back in his relationship with God. He acts as if he is negotiating with God,
trying to buy God off. So though he may do many good things,
he keeps running from the better and more honest way to face
the issue.

3. The Third Type—"to do Your will is my desire"   [155]

This person would like to be rid of any attachment which gets in the way of God's call to further life. His whole effort is to be in balance, ready to move in any direction that the call from God may take him. Whatever seems better for the service and praise of God our Lord is his whole desire and choice. Meanwhile, he strives to act in such a way that he seemingly is free of any attachments. He makes efforts neither to want to retain his possessions nor to want to give them away, unless the service and praise of God our Lord is the God-given motivation for his action. As a result, the graced desire to be better able to serve God our Lord is the cause of his accepting or letting go of anything.

COLLOQUY: I make use of the same three colloquies described   [156]
in the preceding meditation on the Two Leaders, Two Strategies.

Note: We may find it helpful at this time of the retreat when   [157]
we might discover some attachment opposed to actual poverty or a repugnance to it, or when we are not indifferent to poverty and riches, to come to Jesus our Lord in prayer and beg him to choose us to serve him in actual poverty. We should beg with a certain insistence, and we should plead for it—but always wanting what God wants for us.

The Fifth Day   [158]

The contemplation on Our Lord's Baptism by John in the Jordan (see no. 40 at [273] below).

FURTHER DIRECTIONS

1. Beginning with the Fifth Day, it is suggested that only one   [159]
Scripture passage be used to provide the prayer material for the entire day. Since the Exercises have as a primary aim the choice of a state or way of life, the purpose in limiting the amount of new material to be considered in prayer is to keep the head less occupied with many thoughts. Within the free time of these days, retreatants may likely be doing much weighing of alternatives, trying to understand the lead of God in their lives. As a result, the director is encouraged to keep the prayer material itself simple and less demanding of much reasoning.

Yet it should be pointed out that the number of prayer periods is maintained, with the usual repetitions leading to the more simple gaze of the Application of the Senses for the same mystery of Christ's life.

It might also be good to recall that even though we speak of a simplifying of the prayer at this time of the retreat, we are still most careful to observe the preparatory reverence and dedication of everything in our day to God, the petition for a specified grace, and the intimate conversation of the colloquy. Because of the intensity of the search for God's will and our response at this period of the retreat, the triple colloquy addressed to Mary, Christ, and the Father might well remain an ordinary part of these prayer periods.

[160]   2. The Particular Examen of Conscience usually made at midday and before retiring should continue its focus on the faults and negligences with regard to the exercises of the day, especially in view of the helps or aids to prayers which have been suggested.

[161]   **The Sixth Day**

The contemplation on Christ our Lord's being led into the

desert to be tempted (see no. 41 at [274] below).

The Seventh Day

The contemplation on Jesus' calls to the apostles (see no. 42 at [275] below).

The Eighth Day

The contemplation on the Eight Beatitudes (see no. 45 at [272] below).

The Ninth Day

The contemplation on Christ's walking on the water (see no. 47 at [280] below).

The Tenth Day

The contemplation on Jesus preaching in the temple (see no. 55 at [288] below).

The Eleventh Day

The contemplation on Jesus' raising of Lazarus (see no. 52 at [285] below).

The Twelfth Day

The contemplation on the triumphal entry into Jerusalem (see no. 54 at [287] below).

FURTHER DIRECTIONS

1. The Second Week, similar to the First, has no set number [162] of days. According to the progress of the retreatant, especially in view of a choice which one is trying to clarify, the director may want to lengthen or shorten the Week.

In lengthening the Week, the director might suggest other mysteries from the infancy narratives in the Gospels, such as the Visitation of Mary to Elizabeth, the Shepherds at Bethlehem, the Circumcision of the Child Jesus, and the Three Wise Men's Journey and Adoration. By contrast, if the director thinks it well that the Week should be shortened, he may omit some of the mysteries that have been proposed. However many mysteries are taken up in the Second Week, they only serve to introduce the retreatant into a way of prayer which will continue to draw a person more deeply into the life of Christ our Lord.

2. If a retreatant is trying to clarify a choice of a state or [163] way of life, the time for this consideration begins with the Fifth Day, where the contemplation of Our Lord's own setting forth to the Jordan determines the vocation of his own public life.

3. Before I as a retreatant enter into my considerations about [164] the choice of a state or way of life, it is very useful to spend some time mulling over the following description of Three Kinds of Humility. These are thought over from time to time outside of the formal prayer periods from the Fifth Day onward. Perhaps after a day or two of consideration, I may find that I want

to be gifted in the way most expressive of my love and dedication to Jesus Christ, my Lord and God. Then I should make use of the threefold colloquy to manifest the intensity of my desire for this grace.

THREE KINDS OF HUMILITY

Humility lies in the acceptance of Jesus Christ as the fullness of what it means to be human. To be humble is to live as close to the truth as possible: that I am created to the likeness of Christ, that I am meant to live according to the pattern of his paschal mystery, and that my whole fulfillment is found in being as near to Christ as he draws me to himself. The following descriptions try to sum up three different general areas on the spectrum of humility as it is actually lived by men and women.

[165]   1. The First Kind of Humility. This is living out the truth which is necessary for salvation, and so it describes one extreme of the spectrum. I would want to do nothing that would cut me off from God—not even were I made head of all creation or even just to save my own life here on earth. I know that grave sin in this sense is to miss the whole meaning of being a person— one who is created and redeemed and is destined to live forever in love with God my Creator and Lord.

[166]   2. The Second Kind of Humility. This kind is more perfect than the first, and so we find ourselves somewhere along the middle of the spectrum. My life is firmly grounded in the fact that the reality of being a person is seen fully in Jesus Christ. Just as "I have come to do your will, O God" is the motivating force of his life, so the only real principle of choice in my life is to seek out and do the will of my Father. With this habitual attitude, I find that I can maintain a certain balance in my inclinations to have riches rather than poverty, honor rather than dishonor, or to desire a long life rather than a short life. I would not want to turn away from God even in small ways, because my whole desire is to respond ever more faithfully to his call.

[167]   3. The Third Kind of Humility. This is close to the other end of the spectrum, since it demands the understanding and action of a greater grace-gift. It consists in this. I so much want the truth of Christ's life to be fully the truth of my own that I find myself, moved by grace, with a love and a desire for poverty in order to be with the poor Christ; a love and a desire for insults

in order to be closer to Christ in his own rejection by people; a love and a desire to be considered worthless and a fool for Christ, rather than to be esteemed as wise and prudent according to the standards of the world. By grace, I find myself so moved to follow Jesus Christ in the most intimate union possible, that his experiences are reflected in my own. In that, I find my delight.

Note: If after some time for consideration I as a retreatant [168] want to move more in the direction of this third kind of humility, it will help much to make use of the threefold colloquy, as it has been explained above. I should beg our Lord to choose me for the gift of this third kind of humility in order that I may find my own life more patterned according to Jesus, my God and Lord—always, of course, if this is to be for the greater praise and service of God.

INTRODUCTION TO MAKING A CHOICE [169]

OF A STATE OR WAY OF LIFE

In making a choice or in coming to a decision, only one thing is really important—to seek and to find what God calls me to at this time of my life. I know that his call remains faithful; he has created me for himself and my salvation is found in that love. All my choices, then, must be consistent with this given direction of my life.

It becomes obvious how easy it is for me to forget such a simple truth as the end and goal of my whole existence when I consider the manner in which choices are often made. Many people, for example, choose marriage, which is a means, and only secondarily consider the service of God our Lord in marriage, though to do the will of God is each person's end and goal. Many people first choose to make a lot of money or to be successful, and only afterwards to be able to serve God by it. And so too in their striving for power, popularity, and so on. All of these people exhibit an attitude of putting God into second place, and they want God to come into their lives only after their own disordered attachment. In other words, they mix up the order of an end and a means to that end. What they ought to seek first and above all else, they often put last.

It is good, then, for me to recall that my whole aim in life should be to seek to serve God in whatever way his call may come to me. Keeping clearly before me my desire to serve God our Lord, I can begin to search out the means of marrying or not marrying, a life of business involvement or a life of simple frugality, and the like, for these are all means to accomplishing the end. I will choose to use or not use such means only through the inspiration and movement of God's grace leading me on in his service and to my own salvation.

[170]

MATTERS ABOUT WHICH A CHOICE

SHOULD BE MADE

The purpose of these observations is to provide a certain basic information on the matters about which decisions are very important. It contains four points and a note.

1. When we are making a decision or choice, we are not deliberating about choices which involve sin, but rather we are considering alternatives which are lawful and good within our Catholic Church and not bad or opposed to her.

[171]   2. There are choices which represent permanent commitment such as marriage, priesthood, and religious life. There are other choices which can be changed, such as a seeking after a successful career in business or medicine, or a decision to live according to a certain life style.

[172]   3. With regard to a permanent commitment already made, our basic attitude should be that the only choice still called for is the full-hearted gift of self to this state of life. Only this is to be noted. If it becomes apparent that the choice or decision has not been made as it should have been and if there has been a certain disordered attachment involved, our first response is one of sorrow and an attempt to amend by putting our efforts into righting the situation. Professional help or the help of friends who can be objective, along with legitimate authority itself, must oftentimes play an important role at this time of reevaluation.

There is no sense trying to say God's call is directly involved in a choice which we have made because of a disordered attachment. For the call from God is not at the whim of faulty information, sensual emotion, or disordered love.

4. When we are dealing with matters which can be changed, [173] there is no reason to feel anxiety or to move to an unhealthy introspection if we seem to have come to the decision properly and in good order when we first made it. Our one desire should be to find our continued growth in the way of life we have chosen.

Note: If we have poorly come to a decision in matters that [174] are changeable, we should try to make a choice in the proper way whether it would be maintaining the same pattern of life or it would demand a change. For our desire is to praise and serve God in all our choices so that he can continue to work through us for the good of our fellowmen and our world.

THREE TIMES WHEN A CORRECT AND GOOD CHOICE [175]

OF A STATE OR WAY OF LIFE

MAY BE MADE

1. First Time. There is a time of clarity which comes with undeviating persistence. We think of the dramatic change in St. Paul on the road to Damascus, for once he began to respond to the Jesus whom he had been persecuting he never hesitated. From the brief description of Matthew's call in the Gospel, we could draw a similar example. We can feel very gifted when God's call is so unmistakably focused in its drawing power, for this is the best of times for decisions.

2. Second Time. Quite frequently we experience a time of [176] alternating certainties and doubts, of exhilarating strength and debilitating weakness, of consolation and of desolation. As a matter of fact, this time is very privileged, because the discernment of spirits which is called for is an entrance into understanding a language of God spoken within our very being. We can gain much light and understanding from the experience of consolation and desolation, and so this time, too, is very special for correct decision-making.

3. Third Time. Sometimes, through no fault of our own, noth- [177] ing seems to be going on. We are placid, having neither the peace of God's consolation nor the desolation of feeling his absence. It is at this time that we can still think quite clearly

and since we can distinguish no movement from God, we would describe this time as one of our own reasoning process.

We should recall our earlier consideration about ends and means (see [169] above), and so the approach is always within the context of a choice leading to a greater service of God and so for our own salvation. The free and peaceful use of our reasoning abilities shows forth the calm logic of this time.

[178]   If a choice is not made within circumstances as described in the First or Second Times, then some helpful hints at proceeding during the time of calm rationality are given according to two patterns as follows:

A. First Pattern of Making a Good and Correct Choice:

    1. Clearly place before my mind what it is I want to decide about.

[179]   2. Try to be like a balance at equilibrium, without leaning to either side. My end is always clearly before me, but I want to be as free toward the object of my choice as I possibly can be.

[180]   3. Pray that God our Lord enlighten and move me in the way leading to his praise and glory. Then I should use my understanding to weigh the matter carefully and attempt to come to a decision consonant with my living out God's will in my life.

[181]   4. List and weigh the advantages and the disadvantages for me of the various dimensions of my proposed decision.

[182]   5. Consider now which alternative seems more reasonable. Then I will decide according to the more weighty motives and not from my selfish or sensual inclination.

[183]   6. Having come to the decision, I now turn to God again and ask him to accept and confirm it if it is for his greater service and glory by bringing it into the ambit of the Second or First Time.

B. Second Pattern of Making a Correct and Good Choice: [184]

1. Since the love of God should motivate my life, I should check myself whether the greater or less attachment for the object of choice is solely because of my Creator and Lord.

2. I present myself with a person whom I have never met   [185]
before, but who has sought my help in his attempt to respond better to God's call to him. I see what I would tell him, and then I observe the advice which I would so readily give to another for whom I want the best.

3. If I were at the moment of death and so I would have   [186]
the freedom and clarity of that time, what would be the decision I would want to have made now? I will guide myself by this insight and make my present decision in conformity with it.

4. I see myself standing before Christ my Judge when this   [187]
life has ended, and I find myself talking with him about the decision which I have made at this moment in my life. I choose now the course of action which I feel will give me happiness and joy in presenting it to Christ on the day of judgment.

Note: Even after proceeding according to the circumstances   [188]
outlined above, I will take the decision which I have reached by these approaches and beg God our Lord to accept and confirm it if it is for his greater service and glory by bringing it into the ambit of the Second or First Time.

[189]   SOME DIRECTIONS FOR THE RENEWAL OF

OR RECOMMITMENT TO A STATE

OR WAY OF LIFE ALREADY CHOSEN

Often in retreat I find myself not so much faced with the question of a new decision, but rather with the living out of a choice already made. This can be as true of the permanent state of life represented in marriage or priesthood as of the more changeable way of life represented in particular jobs or positions.

During the course of the Exercises, it may be quite profitable to take stock of how my living out of a particular means which I have chosen is truly responding to the faithful call of God. The service and love of God and of neighbor should shine out in my dedication. At this time, I should deepen the attitudes and search out the ways which will better enable me to live the Christ-life in my own surroundings and environment. For my progress in living out my life in Christ will be in proportion to the surrender of my own self-love and of my own will and interests.

THE THIRD WEEK

The First Day and The First Contemplation: [190]

The Last Supper

PREPARATION: I take time to make the usual preparatory reverence and to petition that God direct everything in my day more and more to his praise and service.

GRACE: The gift I seek from God is his allowing me to enter [193] into a sorrow and shame as I stay with Christ in his sufferings borne on my behalf and because of my sins.

THE SETTING: To enter as fully as I can into the preparations [191, for the Passover Meal and into the whole event we call the Last 192, Supper is my purpose in this contemplation. It goes beyond pic- 194, turing the scene or reading the account in words. I try to listen to the way words are spoken, I attempt to see the expression on 195, the face, I am present with as heightened an awareness as I can 196, muster, so that I enter into the mystery I am contemplating. The 197] Gospel accounts depict the preparations, the Supper itself, Christ's washing of the feet of his Apostles, his giving of his Body and Blood in the Eucharist, and his final words to them.

In addition, during this Third Week, I should make even greater effort to labor with Christ through all his anguish, his struggle, his suffering, or what he desires to suffer. At the time of the Passion, I should pay special attention to how the divinity hides itself so that Jesus seems so utterly human and helpless. To realize that Christ loves me so much that he willingly suffers everything for my rejections and sins makes me ask: What can I, in response, do for him?

COLLOQUY: I speak to Jesus, my Lord and Savior, and stay [198]

[199]   with him through everything that happens. I close the period with an Our Father.

Note: Because of the intimacy involved during the contemplations of the Passion, it might be well to review some aspects of the time called "colloquy." Just as in human situations of taking care of the sick or of ministering to the dying, our presence is often more important than our faltering words or awkward actions, so too *to be with* Christ in his Passion describes our prayer response at this time better than any words or actions. Previously we described the colloquy as the intimate conversation between friends. Now we open out that description to include the depth of feeling, love, and compassion, which allows us just *to be there*.

Sometimes, still, we may want to pour out our consolations, our temptations, our fears, our hardness of heart to Christ our Lord. In times of great need, we may find the intensity of our begging reflected in our use of the threefold colloquy. We should remember that faced with the suffering of the Passion we may have to pray even for the gift of letting ourselves want to experience it with Christ, according to the manner suggested after the Meditation on the Three Types of Persons, in the Note at [157] above.

[200]   ## The Second Contemplation

The Agony in the Garden

PREPARATION: I take the time to make the usual preparatory reverence and dedication of my day.

[203]   GRACE: I continue to pray for the gift of being able to feel sorrow with Christ in sorrow, to be anguished with Christ's anguish, and even to experience tears and deep grief because of all the afflictions which Christ endures for me.

[201, 202]   THE SETTING: The Gospels give the details of the event: Christ and his disciples leaving the Upper Room to go towards the garden of Gethsemani. There Jesus takes Peter, James, and John, and goes apart to pray. He experiences such turmoil of spirit that his sweat becomes as drops of blood. Waking his sleepy disciples, he faces the mob, is identified by the kiss of Judas, and is led away to the house of Annas. I labor to enter as fully into the account as I possibly can.

FURTHER DIRECTIONS [204]

1. The second contemplation, as well as all that follow, is done after the manner of the first contemplation dealing with the Last Supper. During the Third Week, two Scripture passages are given for each day, so that the usual repetitions are made, leading to the Application of the Senses as the final period of prayer.

2. Depending upon the age, the health, and the condition of [205] the retreatant, five exercises a day are encouraged, but fewer may be more desirable because of particular circumstances.

3. In the Third Week, some modifications must again be made [206] in the helps for prayer.

Because of the subject matter of the Passion, I make an effort while rising and dressing to be sad and solemn because of the great sorrow and suffering of Christ our Lord.

Throughout the day, I am careful not to bring up pleasant thoughts, even though they are good and holy, as for example thoughts about the Resurrection and life of glory. Rather I try to maintain a certain attitude of sorrow and anguish by calling to mind frequently the labors, fatigue, and suffering which Christ our Lord endured from the time of his birth down to the particular mystery of the Passion which I am presently contemplating.

In a similar way, the Particular Examen of Conscience should [207] be applied to the exercises and my observation of the helps applicable to this Week, just as it was done in the past Weeks.

The Second Day [208]

1. The contemplation on events from the Garden to the house of Annas (see no. 58 at [291] below).

2. The contemplation on events from the house of Annas to the house of Caiaphas (see no. 59 at [292] below). The usual repetitions should be made, with the Application of the Senses being the final prayer period of the day.

The Third Day

1. The contemplation on events from the house of Caiaphas to the house of Pilate (see no. 60 at [293] below).

2. The contemplation on events from the house of Pilate to the palace of Herod (see no. 61 at [294] below). Then the repetitions and Application of the Senses are to be done as noted at [204] above.

The Fourth Day

1. The contemplation on events from Herod's palace back to the house of Pilate (see no. 62 at [295] below).

2. The contemplation on events with Pilate (see no. 62 at [295]). The same procedure should be followed for the repetitions and the Application of the Senses.

The Fifth Day

1. The contemplation on events from the house of Pilate to the crucifixion (see no. 63 at [296] below).

2. The contemplation on events from the raising of the Cross to Jesus' death (see no. 64 at [297] below). The repetitions follow as usual, along with the Application of the Senses.

The Sixth Day

1. The contemplation on events from the taking down from the Cross to the burial (see no. 65 at [298]).

2. The contemplation on events from the burial to Mary's waiting in sorrow.

The repetitions follow as usual, along with the Application of the Senses.

The Seventh Day

1. The contemplation on events of the whole Passion.

2. A repetition on the whole of the Passion. In place of formal

prayer periods, I let the effect of Christ's death permeate my being and the world around me for the rest of the day. I consider the desolation of Our Lady, her great sorrow and weariness, and also that of the disciples.

Note: If we want to spend more time on the Passion, the mysteries can be so divided that, for example, only the Supper is considered in one prayer period, then Christ's washing of the feet of his Apostles in another, next the institution of the Eucharist, and finally the farewell discourse of Christ. The other mysteries which make up the total Passion account could be similarly divided up.   [209]

After the Passion has been contemplated in its various mysteries over some days, there is the possibility of taking one full day on the first half of the Passion, and a second day on the other half, and a final day reviewing the whole of the Passion.

But if we wish to spend less time on the Passion, we could use a different mystery for each of the prayer periods, eliminating all repetitions and Applications of the Senses. After we have finished contemplating the Passion in this way, we could spend one more day just letting the Passion in its whole sweep pervade our day. In all these suggested approaches, the good progress of the retreat is always the guiding consideration.

[210]   GUIDELINES WITH REGARD TO EATING

Preliminary Note: As I begin to grow in my knowledge of Jesus Christ and union with him through the exercises of the Second and Third Weeks, it is clear that the "sense of Christ" is meant to permeate my whole being and all my activities. To reflect on the daily and commonplace activity of eating is to emphasize how total is my response to follow Jesus Christ. As St. Paul says, "whether you eat or drink—whatever you do—you should do all for the glory of God" (1 Cor. 10:31).

The following guidelines, then, are meant to model a reflective approach about my conduct in every part of my life so that being ever more fully penetrated by the life of Christ within me, I show forth a proper ordering of the various areas of my life. In the words of St. Paul, "whatever you do, work at it with your whole being" (Col. 3:23). Through such guidelines, I can begin even now to live out the reordering process which has begun to be effected in me during the course of the retreat. I also look forward to the time after the retreat when these guidelines are meant to be an integral part of my life.

A. *General Principle*

[214]   1. It is while I am eating that I should reflect upon Christ and his apostles at table. I should try to enter into the presence of Christ so fully that I have a sense of how Jesus eats and drinks, how he speaks and handles himself in the context of a meal. Even at the very time of doing this exercise of the imagination, I will find that I no longer have the food itself as a focus of my attention. As a result, I will come to a greater order in my own conduct at table, perhaps both in what I eat and in how I act while eating.

B. *Particular Applications*

[210]   2. There seems to be less problem for a proper ordering in my life when it is a matter of bread or the ordinary staples of diet.

[211]   3. There does seem to be a greater care necessary when I consider the area of drink. Whatever the beverage—beer, soda, coffee, milk, wine, and so on—I should consider what is helpful and so pursue the proper moderation for myself, and also what may be harmful and so avoid the disordered excess.

4. When I consider the wide variety of food available to me, [212]
I should be more conscious of its appeal to my appetites and so
of the necessity for a greater sense of control. To avoid disorder
concerning foods, a certain abstinence can be practiced in two
ways:

(a) by seeking out less delicate foods, even to a greater
dependence on the staples within the diet;

(b) by eating sparingly of rich and delicate foods.

5. It is good to discover a proper mean for myself in my eating [213]
habits. While taking care not to fall sick, I can reduce my intake
of food in order to come to such a mean. There are two reasons
why seeking such a mean can be profitable:

(a) commonly the observation of a mean in my diet provides a disposition whereby I will often experience
more abundant lights, consolations, and divine movements within my spirit. These experiences, in turn, may
confirm me in the ordering of such a mean in eating;

(b) when I discover that observing a certain chosen mean
in diet brings about an inability to continue well in the
performance of the exercises of the retreat, I will then
come more easily to adjust such a mean in order that
I can have the necessary strength and health for my
ordinary daily life and activity.

C. *Particular Attitudes*

6. In regard to my attention at a meal time, I may find a read- [215]
ing about a saint or a particular spiritual apostolate very helpful
in fixing my focus beyond the mere gratification of my hunger.
Music, too, can provide a reflective and relaxed setting for meals.

7. If the whole focus of my attention at meals is upon food [216]
itself, I can find that I am carried away by my appetites. I may
also discover that I am bolting my food so hurriedly that there
is little evidence of a Christ-behavior in my activity of eating
a meal. Both in the amount of food eaten and in the way it is
eaten, I should be ordering my life in Christ.

8. If I were to plan ahead for my meals, I may find that an [217]
order in my eating habits is far easier to accomplish. For example, it can be very helpful after lunch or after dinner or at a time
when I do not feel a desire for food to determine how much I
will eat at the next meal. Then at the time of the meal itself, I
should not exceed that amount which I set myself, no matter
how strong the temptation might be. In fact, if I find myself
strongly moved by my appetites to eat more, I should take even
less than the amount I had predetermined.

THE FOURTH WEEK

[218]   **The First Day and the First Contemplation:**

            the Appearance of Christ our Lord to Mary

            PREPARATION: I take the time for the usual preparatory rev-
            erence and petition that God direct everything in my day more
            and more to his praise and service.

[221]   GRACE: I beg for the gift of being able to enter into the joy
            and consolation of Jesus in the victory of his risen life.

[219,   THE SETTING: In the usual way, I try to enter into this con-
 220,   templation as fully as I can. Although I do not have a Scripture
            account to guide my thoughts, I can easily know the excitement
 222,   of Jesus in wanting to share the joy of his resurrection with his
 223,   Mother who had stood by him throughout the Passion. I let the
 224]   delight and the love of this encounter permeate my being.

            In contrast to the Passion, I should note how much the di-
            vinity shines through the person of Christ in all his appearances.
            The peace and the joy which he wants to share with me can only
            be a gift of God. To realize that the role of consoler which Christ
            performs in each of his resurrection appearances is the same role
            he performs now in my life is a faith insight into why I can live
            my life in a true Christian optimism.

[225]   COLLOQUY: According to the circumstances of the setting, I
            let my response be directed to one or more persons or let it be in
            the threefold manner to Mary, Christ, and the Father. In every
            case, I always close the prayer period with an Our Father.

FURTHER DIRECTIONS

1. In all the contemplations of this Fourth Week—the mys- [226] teries of the Resurrection through the Ascension inclusive, the usual procedure should be followed as was done in the previous Week. A shortening or lengthening of the Week can easily be made by a selection or division of the various mysteries. The freedom shown in the Week on the Passion should be the guide.

2. Ordinarily it is more in keeping with the atmosphere of re- [227] laxed consolation in this Week to have no more than four periods of prayer within the day, although there could be three passages of Scripture presented for contemplation. As a result, the pattern of prayer periods begins with the one upon arising in the morning, the second later in the morning, the third sometime in the afternoon, and the fourth period, which is usually described as the Application of the Senses, in the evening.

This fourth period of prayer centers on those aspects of the preceding three contemplations where the retreatant was more moved and there was greater spiritual relish.

3. As I allow the Scripture passage to present me with the set- [228] ting for prayer, I know that certain elements provide me with a focus. I should be sure to let these focal points direct my attention during the prayer period so that the general good feeling of this Week with its possible distractions or scattering of attention does not mitigate my response to the Lord.

4. In the Fourth Week, I make some modifications in the helps [229] toward making the whole day consistently prayerful.

As soon as I awake, I recall the atmosphere of joy which pervades this Week and review the particular mystery about which I am to contemplate.

Throughout the day, I try to keep myself in a mood which is marked by happiness and spiritual joy. As a result, anything in my environment—the sun and warm weather or the white cover of snow, all the different beauties of nature, and so on—is used to reinforce the atmosphere of consolation.

Obviously, during this period, penance is not in keeping with the total movement, and so only the usual temperance and moderation in all things is encouraged.

[230]   CONTEMPLATION ON THE LOVE OF GOD

Preliminary Note: Before this exercise is presented, two observations should be made:

[231]
(1) the first is that love ought to show itself in deeds over and above words;

(2) the second is that love consists in a mutual sharing of goods. For example, a lover gives and shares with the beloved something of his personal gifts or some possession which he has or is able to give; so, too, the beloved shares with the lover. In this way, one who has knowledge shares it with one who does not, and this is true for honors, riches, and so on. In love, one always wants to give to the other.

PREPARATION: I take the usual time to place myself reverently in the presence of my Lord and my God, and beg that God will direct everything in my day more and more to his praise and service.

[232]   At this time, I may find it especially helpful to imagine myself standing before God and all his saints who are praying for me.

[233] GRACE: I beg for the gift of an intimate knowledge of all the sharing of goods which God does in his love for me. Filled with gratitude, I want to be empowered to respond just as totally in my love and service of him.

THE SETTING: There are four different focal points which present the subject matter for my prayer:

[234] 1. God's gifts to me.

God creates me out of love which desires nothing more than a return of love on my part. So much does he love me that even though I take myself away from him, he continues to be my Savior and Redeemer.

All my natural abilities and gifts, along with the gifts of Baptism and the Eucharist and the special graces lavished upon me, are only so many signs of how much God our Lord shares his life with me. My consolation: who I am by the grace of God!

If I were to respond as a reasonable person, what could I give in return to such a Lover? Moved by love, I may want to express my own love-response in the following words:

TAKE AND RECEIVE

Take, Lord, and receive all my liberty, my memory, my understanding, and my entire will—all that I have and call my own. You have given it all to me. To you, Lord, I return it. Everything is yours; do with it what you will. Give me only your love and your grace. That is enough for me.

2. God's gift of himself to me. [235]

God not only gives gifts to me, but he literally gives himself to me. His is not only the Word in whom all things are created, but also the Word who becomes flesh and dwells with us. He gives himself to me so that his Body and Blood become the food and drink of my life. He pours out upon me his Spirit so that I can cry out "Abba." God loves me so much that I literally become a dwelling-place or a temple of God—growing in an ever deepening realization of the image and likeness of God which remains the glory of the creation of man and woman.

If I were to make only a reasonable response, what could I do? Moved by love, I may find that I can respond best in words like the TAKE AND RECEIVE.

3. God's labors for me. [236]

God loves me so much that he enters into the very struggle of life. Like a potter with clay, like a mother in childbirth, or like a mighty force blowing life into dead bones, God labors to share his life and his love. His labors take him even to death on a cross in order to bring forth the life of the Resurrection.

Once more I question myself how I can make a response. Let me look again to the expression of the TAKE AND RECEIVE.

[237]   4. God as Giver and Gift.

God's love shines down upon me like the light rays from the sun, or his love is poured forth lavishly like a fountain spilling forth its waters into an unending stream. Just as I see the sun in its rays and the fountain in its waters, so God pours forth himself in all the gifts which he showers upon me. His delight and his joy is to be with the sons of men—to be with me. He cannot do enough to speak out his love for me—ever calling me to a fuller and better life.

What can I respond to such a generous Giver? Let me consider once again the expression of the TAKE AND RECEIVE.

I close the prayer with an Our Father.

Note: There are a number of approaches which we can use as we pray this Contemplation on the Love of God.

The Contemplation could provide the prayer material for the final day or days of the Fourth Week and so close out the retreat. All four points of the Contemplation could be used in a single prayer period. Then the repetitions would continue to simplify the response throughout the prayer periods of the day. Perhaps one or two points of the Contemplation might provide the material for the whole day, with the usual repetitions being employed.

Another approach would be to use the Contemplation as a whole or with any one of its points as the final prayer period of each day within the Fourth Week, taking the place of the usual Application of the Senses. Perhaps one final day would be spent upon the total material of the Contemplation, after the manner of reviewing the whole of the Passion in the Third Week.

Whatever is more conducive to the good closure of the retreat for the particular retreatant is the determining guide for how to proceed.

Preliminary Note. St. Ignatius of Loyola was anxious to help people to continue to develop their prayer lives. He outlines briefly some ways of praying which we can use when we have no text of Scripture at hand, when we are tired or travelling, or when in general we are left to our own resources. Although there are many far more developed treatises on prayer, Ignatius' simple directives can still be helpful to us today.

A. THE FIRST METHOD OF PRAYING

The first method of praying deals with the matter of the ten commandments, or the seven deadly sins, or the three powers of the soul, or the five senses of the body. What will be described is the preparation for the time of prayer and the ways of moving into the consideration of the matter. The actual praying we will not attempt to formulate.

I. *On the Ten Commandments*

PREPARATION: Before entering into the time for praying, we [239] spend some time relaxing, either by sitting or by walking. It is good to take this time to recall what we are about to do. To make this preparation time is important for entering well into all methods of praying.

GRACE: Next we speak out our need for a particular grace from [240] God our Lord: begging that we may know how we have failed in keeping the ten commandments, that we might be able to come to a better understanding of them, and that we might be more capable of living them out, to the greater glory and praise of God.

THE METHOD: In order to enter into the first method of pray- [241] ing, it is good to reflect upon how we have been faithful and how we have failed in our observance of the first commandment. In the brief time that we center our attention on the first commandment, we may become aware of our failings and so we ask pardon and forgiveness of them from God. Before moving on to the next commandment, we will say an Our Father. And so in this same way, we take up each commandment for consideration and for prayer.

[242]   Note 1. If we find that we have no failings in regard to a particular commandment, we will move on more quickly to the next one to be considered. But if we find that a particular commandment is very central to our Christian living, we may need to spend more time in consideration. This way of proceeding remains helpful when we take up the matter of the deadly sins.

[243]   Note 2. When we have finished our reflections upon all the commandments, both in asking forgiveness and in begging the grace to respond better in the future, we spend the time speaking intimately with God our Lord and saying whatever comes to our mind and from our heart in regard to the particular matter which we have considered in our prayer.

[244]   II. *On the Deadly Sins:* (pride, anger, envy, lust
                          gluttony, avarice, sloth)

THE METHOD: The second area which provides matter for this method of praying is a consideration of the deadly sins. We should proceed in the same way as we did in regard to the matter of the commandments. After an initial relaxation time and preparatory prayer for the grace which we are seeking, we move into the consideration of the deadly sins. In contrast with the commandments which are to be faithfully observed, we are now reflecting upon sins or patterns of behavior which are to be avoided. But otherwise our way of proceeding remains the same, with a short time spent in reflecting on each sin, asking forgiveness for failures, saying an Our Father, and so passing through all the sins until we have our final time of intimate prayer with God our Lord.

[245]   Note: In order to enter more deeply into the consideration of the seven deadly sins, we should also review the seven virtues which are their contraries. We should pray to grow in these virtues and observe them ever more faithfully.

III. *On the Three Powers of the Soul*   [246]
    (memory, understanding, will)

THE METHOD: A third area which may be proposed as matter for this method of praying is a consideration of the three powers of the soul. Once again the same procedure is followed: a short time for relaxation and recollection, then a preparatory prayer for the grace which we are seeking, the consideration of the matter itself with its time of begging, thanking, praising, or asking forgiveness, and a closing out of the period of prayer with a final intimate speaking to the Lord.

IV. *On the Five Senses of the Body*   [247]

THE METHOD: A fourth area which may be proposed as matter for this method of praying is a consideration of the five bodily senses. The way of proceeding in the prayer period remains the same, with only the change in the matter being considered.

Note: Because we may want to imitate Christ our Lord in the [248] use of our senses, we might begin by placing ourselves humbly before God our Lord in our preparation time. As we consider each sense, we say either one Hail Mary or one Our Father. We may wish, however, to pray to imitate Our Lady in the use of our senses. In our preparation time, we place ourselves before her and beg that she may obtain for us this very grace from her Son and Lord, Then after we consider each sense, we say one Hail Mary.

B. THE SECOND METHOD OF PRAYING   [249]

The second method of praying centers upon contemplating the meaning of each word in a traditional prayer formula.

PREPARATION: We always observe the time interval in which [250] we relax and reflect upon what we are about to do.

GRACE: The preparatory prayer in which we beg for a par- [251] ticular grace is addressed to the person who is the subject of the traditional prayer which we are considering.

THE METHOD: We can understand the second method of [252] praying in the following way. We use the Our Father as our example. Our position during such prayer can be kneeling or sitting, whichever seems to be more conducive to praying and better fitted to our own devotion. We take care to keep our attention focused in this method of praying by taking advantage of a help like keeping our eyes closed or fixing our gaze upon some one place or object. As we begin our consideration, we say "Father," and we let this word remain within us for so long a time as we find meanings, comparisons, relish, and consolation coming from our reflection upon this word. We act in a similar way with every word of the Our Father or of any prayer we may **want to pray in this method.**

[253]   Rule 1. We fill out our time for prayer by reflecting on each word of a prayer we have chosen, and then we close out the time by saying the Hail Mary, the Creed, the Soul of Christ, and the Hail Holy Queen, aloud or not, in the usual way.

[254]   Rule 2. We observe that when one word or two of the prayer, Our Father, occupies our full attention with relish and consolation, we do not hurry on. Rather we remain where we find devotion even though the full time for praying elapses in this way. When we have come to the end of our prayer period, we simply pray the rest of the Our Father in the usual way.

[255]   Rule 3. We may spend a whole hour of prayer on one word or two of the Our Father. If we wish to continue using this method of praying on successive days, we can then say the words which we have previously prayed over in the usual way, and on the next word which follows we can once more begin to contemplate according to this second method.

[256]   Note 1: We may spend some days in praying the Our Father according to this second method. We could then use the Hail Mary, and continue on with other traditional prayers so that this method of praying can remain a helpful pattern for our life of prayer.

[257]   Note 2: When this second method of praying is used, we bring the time of prayer to completion by turning to the person to whom we have addressed our petition for grace, and in a brief manner plead now the more fervently for the virtues or graces which we feel that we most need.

C. THE THIRD METHOD OF PRAYING [258]

The third method of praying consists in our making use of a certain rhythmical flow.

PREPARATION: We take the usual time to relax and reflect upon what we are about to do.

GRACE: We make the preparatory prayer in which we beg for a particular grace by addressing the person who is the subject of the particular vocal prayer which we are using.

THE METHOD: The third method of praying can be described in the following way. We are so relaxed that our breathing in and out comes at a slow but steady pace. If we use the Our Father, we say one word at a time while we breathe in and out. And so with the next breath, we say or take up the next word. In the interval of time which takes place in our breathing in and out, we look mainly to the meaning of the word, or to the person whom we are addressing, or to our own neediness, or to the difference between the holiness of God and his saints and our own sinfulness. In this way, we proceed word by word through the Our Father. To fill out the time set aside for our prayer, we could then say other prayers in our ordinary way—prayers such as the Hail Mary, Soul of Christ, the Creed, and the Hail Holy Queen.

Rule 1. If on another day or at another time in the same day [259] we want to pray more according to this third method, we can then use the Hail Mary. Again we proceed word by word in the same rhythmical flow of breathing. All the traditional vocal prayers of the Church are available for us to use in this way.

Rule 2. If we find that we have the time and that we work [260] well with this third method of praying, we can use one prayer and, upon completing it, move on to another and so proceed throughout the whole prayer period, always keeping the same rhythmical flow of breathing for each one of the prayers which we consider.

SCRIPTURE TEXTS

FOR

THE FOUNDATION: FACT AND PRACTICE

Preliminary Note: Although St. Ignatius of Loyola did not suggest any Scripture texts during the time for considering The Foundation, or even during the meditations of the First Week, it is a common practice to approach or reinforce this material through the use of Scripture.

Some suggested texts are presented for this early part of the Exercises in a manner that is consistent with the Ignatian presentation for the Second, Third, and Fourth Weeks. The texts presented are to be used or not, always in view of the needs of a particular retreatant and the abilities of an individual retreat director. Different texts, as well as additional texts, are possible because the only criterion is always the good progress of this particular retreatant.

In the Second, Third, and Fourth Weeks, the Scripture texts given below are those suggested by St. Ignatius himself.

A. Some suggested Scripture Texts for the Foundation:

1. MAN IS CREATED

Psalm 103

Focus: how good God is to mankind

Note: When praying a psalm, a number of approaches can be used:
(1) very slowly reading through the psalm, making it one's prayer expression; or
(2) letting certain lines or phrases hold one's attention for the whole period of prayer; or
(3) thoughtfully reading through the psalm a number of times within the prayer period.

2. GOD THE CREATOR
Psalm 104
Focus: how great God is.

3. THE LORD, OUR GOD
Psalm 105
Focus: how faithful God is to mankind.

4. GRATITUDE TO GOD
Psalm 136
Focus: the mantra-like response is made to every thought about God—"For his mercy endures forever."

5. THE CREATION OF MAN
Genesis 1-2:4
Focus: a good creation has men and women at its center.

6. THE WORD IN CREATION
John 1:1-14
Focus: God's Word is the center and source of all life.

7. THE NEARNESS OF GOD
Psalm 139
Focus: how well God knows me and how close he is to me.

8. GOD INVITES US
Isaiah 55
Focus: God gives so freely and so effectively.

9. GOD'S DWELLING AMONG MEN
Revelation 21:1-8
Focus: God is always with us in this "new earth."

10. CHRIST AS SOURCE OF ALL LIFE
Colossians 1:15-23
Focus: Jesus Christ is the center of creation and our center.

11. WE MUST BE FREE TO RESPOND
Genesis 12:1-9 and Genesis 22:1-18
Focus: Abraham has faith in God's lead.

12. WE MUST BE FREE TO RESPOND
Acts 9:1-19
Focus: Saul surrenders to Christ's lead.

13. WE MUST BE FREE TO RESPOND
Mark 10:17-31
Focus: the following of God's call is free, but costly.

B. Some Suggested Scripture Texts for the First Week:

14. THE FIRST SIN OF MAN
Genesis 3:1-19
Focus: how devastating is one sin and its effect.

15. THE HISTORY OF SIN
Psalm 106
Focus: how many times men continue to reject a loving God.

16. REJECTION OF GOD AS REJECTION OF LIFE
Matthew 13:4-23
Focus: God's seed within us must be nurtured or else death results.

17. RECOGNITION OF SIN
2 Samuel 12:1-15
Focus: how blind a man can be to his own action.

18. EXPERIENCE OF SIN
Romans 7:13-23
Focus: how deep the effects of sin are in us.

19. PERSONAL RESPONSIBILITY FOR SIN
Ezekiel 18:1-32
Focus: "I" am responsible for my choices.

20. SIN CONFESSED BEFORE GOD
Isaiah 59:1-21
Focus: as sinner, I come before my God.

21. SINNER IS WHAT I AM
        1 John 1:5-2:17
    Focus: I am sinner and saved.

22. FORGIVENESS
        Matthew 18:21-35
    Focus: God's forgiveness calls for my own forgiving.

23. JUDGMENT
        Matthew 25:31-46
    Focus: God's compassion sets the pattern for my own compassion.

24. JUDGMENT
        Matthew 7:1-23
    Focus: God's judgment looks to the whole of my life.

25. PRAYER OF A SINNER
        Psalm 38
    Focus: I cry out to God in my need.

26. PRAYER OF REPENTANCE
        Psalm 51
    Focus: I ask for mercy.

27. DEATH TO SIN
        Romans 6
    Focus: Sin is possible, but I choose Christ.

28. THE RAISING OF LAZARUS
        John 11:1-44
    Focus: One who is dead is raised up by Christ.

C. The Mysteries of the Life of Our Lord—Second Week

29. THE ANNUNCIATION TO OUR LADY   [262]
        Luke 1:26-38
    Focus: God's word calls forth Mary's response.

[263]   30. THE VISITATION OF OUR LADY TO ELIZABETH
                    Luke 1:39-56
                Focus: Mary rejoices in being the Christ-
                bearer.

[264]   31. BIRTH OF CHRIST OUR LORD
                    Luke 2:1-14
                Focus: I can simply gaze upon God-become-
                man.

[265]   32. THE SHEPHERDS
                    Luke 2:8-20
                Focus: how the good news affects men.

[266]   33. THE CIRCUMCISION
                    Luke 2:21
                Focus: the name Jesus has so much meaning.

[267]   34. THE MAGI
                    Matthew 2:1-12
                Focus: the great faith called forth in the
                Magi.

[268]   35. THE PURIFICATION OF OUR LADY AND THE
            PRESENTATION OF THE CHILD JESUS
                    Luke 2:22-39
                Focus: the examples of Mary, Jesus, Simeon
                and Anna are each a call to faith.

[269]   36. THE FLIGHT INTO EGYPT
                    Matthew 2:13-18
                Focus:the care of God's providence is made
                evident.

[270]   37. THE RETURN FROM EGYPT
                    Matthew 2:19-23
                Focus:God's work is seen in ordinary human
                decisions.

[271]   38. THE LIFE OF CHRIST OUR LORD FROM THE
            AGE OF TWELVE TO THE AGE OF THIRTY
                    Luke 2:51-52
                Focus: How ordinary is the growth of Jesus.

[281]   48. THE APOSTLES ARE SENT TO PREACH
Matthew 10:1-16
Focus: Jesus shares his mission.

[282]   49. THE CONVERSION OF MAGDALENE
Luke 7:36-50
Focus: Jesus calls to conversion by love.

[283]   50. CHRIST FEEDS THE FIVE THOUSAND
Matthew 14:13-21
Focus: Jesus' concern is shown for all the people.

[284]   51. THE TRANSFIGURATION
Matthew 17:1-9
Focus: Jesus has his own religious experience.

[285]   52. THE RAISING OF LAZARUS
John 11:1-45
Focus: Jesus is seen as the Resurrection and the Life.

[286]   53. THE SUPPER AT BETHANY
Matthew 26:6-10
Focus: Jesus accepts a love gesture.

[287]   54. PALM SUNDAY
Matthew 21:1-17
Focus: Jesus enters Jerusalem as King and Messiah.

[288]   55. JESUS PREACHES IN THE TEMPLE
Luke 19:47-48
Focus: Jesus remains faithful to his mission.

D. The Mysteries of the Life of Our Lord—Third Week:

[289]   56. THE LAST SUPPER
Matthew 26:20-30; John 13:1-30
Focus: Jesus serves in giving himself totally.

[290]   57. FROM THE SUPPER TO THE AGONY INCLUSIVE
Matthew 26:30-46; Mark 14:32-44
Focus: Jesus seeks only the will of his Father.

E. The Mysteries of the Life of Our Lord—Fourth Week:

[299]   66. THE RESURRECTION OF CHRIST OUR
          LORD—THE FIRST APPARITION
                    No Scripture text
                Focus: Jesus is seen in his consoling role for
                Mary his mother.

[300]   67. THE SECOND APPARITION
                         Mark 16:1-11
                Focus: "He is risen."

[301]   68. THE THIRD APPARITION
                         Matthew 28
                Focus: Jesus is the consoler.

[302]   69. THE FOURTH APPARITION
                    Luke 24:9-12 and 33-34
                Focus: how wonderful is the resurrection of
                the Lord.

[303]   70. THE FIFTH APPARITION
                         Luke 24
                Focus: Christ is the consoler.

[304]   71. THE SIXTH APPARITION
                         John 20:19-23
                Focus: Christ is the life-giver.

[305]   72. THE SEVENTH APPARITION
                         John 20:24-29
                Focus: faith in the Lord Jesus is seeing and
                not seeing.

[306]   73. THE EIGHTH APPARITION
                         John 21:1-17
                Focus: Christ is the consoler.

[307]   74. THE NINTH APPARITION
                         Matthew 28:16-20
                Focus: Christ sends out his followers.

GUIDELINES FOR THE DISCERNMENT OF SPIRITS

Preliminary Note: On the use of "spirits," good and evil.

"Discernment of spirits" is a venerable phrase of Christian
spiritual tradition. From the action of good or evil spirits upon
one result "movements of one's heart or spirit," "motions affecting
one's interior life," "a certain impetus in one's life," "a feeling for or
against some course of action," and so on. The descriptive words
"good" and "evil" as applied to "spirits" are used to designate
primarily the source or cause of the movement or feeling as a good
or an evil spirit. What we experience, however, is that good
spirits lead a person in a good direction towards a good goal. Evil
spirits make use of evil directions, and even sometimes of what
are at first good directions, to accomplish an evil end.

Although the importance of these movements comes in the direction which they give to our lives, we are necessarily concerned about recognizing their good or evil source, especially
in view of the possible deception of an apparently good direction. In the light of modern psychology, we have some indi-
cations of the great complexity of human motivations. Added
to this complexity of human motivation, we Christians live in a
faith-world which acknowledges the unfathomable power of evil
personified in Satan and the damned of hell and the even more
mysterious power of good focused in God and in the communion
of saints. And so when we attempt to say something not only
about the direction of these spirits but also about what the
sources of these good and evil spirits or motions are, we can
still find helpful a scheme adapted and expanded from the traditional Ignatian division in [32]:

Good spirits and evil spirits come from
    (1) within our very selves, or
    (2) outside of us, from
       (a) our fellow men, or
       (b) power more than human.

Although as redeemed sinners we can confess that both good
and evil motions emanate from within us, we still stand amazed
at both the good and the evil which comes forth from the heart

of us human beings. Like St. Paul in his seventh chapter of the Letter to the Romans, we suffer from the divisions we feel within our very selves. In fact, we commonly feel more comfortable to be able to blame evil on someone or something outside of ourselves. Even the first sin of man and woman is pictured in such a way in the third chapter of Genesis when Adam attempts to shift the blame to Eve, and Eve looks to the serpent. Yet without in any way lessening our own potential human malice, we have experientially as well as scripturally the evidence of a power of evil that is bigger than any one person or group of persons. Just as our fellowmen can influence our choices and action towards wrong, so too the "more than human" power of evil is destructive and deadly in its enticements and enslavements. While our fellowmen can also be an influence for good, we know similarly from experience and from Scripture another power of good, which comes from God himself directly intervening in our lives as well as the continuing intercession of the saints who have gone before us.

In the following guidelines for discerning spirits, an attempt is made to give helps to develop an ability to recognize ever earlier the direction of certain movements or feelings in our lives, and so to be able to follow or reject them almost in their very sources.

PART I. Guidelines Suitable Especially for the First Week [313-327]

The statements below are an attempt to present certain norms which might be helpful in understanding different interior movements which happen in the "heart" of man and woman. By the grace of God, we are meant to recognize those that are good so that we might let them give direction to our lives and those that are bad so that we might reject them or turn aside from them.

The norms in this first section are more appropriate to the kind of spiritual experiences associated with the First Week of the Exercises.

A. Two Statements of General Application

1. When we are caught up in a life of sin or perhaps even [314] if we are closed off from God in only one area of our life, the evil spirit is ordinarily accustomed to propose a slothful complacency

or a future of ever greater pleasures still to be grasped. He fills our imagination with all kinds of sensual delights so that there is no will or desire to change the evil direction of our life.

The good spirit uses just the opposite method with us. He will try to make us see the absurdity of the direction our life has taken. Little by little an uneasiness described sometimes as the "sting" of conscience comes about and a feeling of remorse sets in.

[315]   2. When we are intent upon living a good life and seeking to pursue the lead of God in our life, the tactics of the spirits are just the opposite of those described above.

The evil spirit proposes to us all the problems and difficulties in living a good life. The evil spirit attempts to rouse a false sadness for things which will be missed, to bring about anxiety about perservering when we are so weak, to suggest innumerable roadblocks in walking the way of the Lord. And so the evil spirit tries discouragement and deception to deter us from growing in the Christ-life.

The good spirit, however, strengthens and encourages, consoles and inspires, establishes a peace and sometimes moves to a firm resolve. To lead a good life gives delight and joy, and no obstacle seems to be so formidable that it cannot be faced and overcome. The good spirit thereby continues an upright person's progress in the Lord.

> B. Particular Statements Referring Especially
> to Persons Intent upon Changing Their Lives
> and Doing Good.

First of all, two terms should be defined:

[316]   3. SPIRITUAL CONSOLATION. This term describes our interior life:
(a) when we find ourselves so on fire with the love of God that neither anything nor anyone presents itself in competition with a total gift of self to God in love. Rather we begin to see everything and everyone in the context of God, their Creator and Lord;
(b) when we are saddened, even to the point of tears, for our infidelity to God but at the same time thankful to know

God as Savior. Such consolation often comes in a deep realization of ourselves as sinner before a God who loves us, or in the face of Christ's Passion when we see that Jesus loves his Father and his fellowmen so much, or for any other reason which leads us to praise and thank and serve God all the better;

(c) when we find our life of faith, hope, and love so strengthened and emboldened that the joy of serving God is foremost in our life. More simply said, consolation can be found in any increase of our faith, our hope, and our love. A deep-down peace comes in just "being in my Father's house."

4. SPIRITUAL DESOLATION. This term describes our in-   [317]
terior life:

(a) when we find ourselves enmeshed in a certain turmoil of spirit or feel ourselves weighed down by a heavy darkness or weight;

(b) when we experience a lack of faith or hope or love in the very distaste for prayer or for any spiritual activity and we know a certain restlessness in our carrying on in the service of God;

(c) when we experience just the opposite effect of what has been described as spiritual consolation. For we will notice that the thoughts of rebelliousness, despair, or selfishness which arise at the time of desolation are in absolute contrast with the thoughts of the praise and service of God which flow during the time of consolation.

> Four guidelines dealing with spiritual desolation now follow:

5. When we find ourselves weighed down by a certain deso-   [318]
lation, we should not try to change a previous decision or to come to a new decision. The reason is that in desolation the evil spirit is making an attempt to obstruct the good direction of our life or to change it, and so we would be thwarted from the gentle lead of God, and what is more conducive to our own salvation. As a result, at a time of desolation, we hold fast to the decision which guided us during the time before the desolation came on us.

6. Although we should not try to make new decisions at a   [319]
time of desolation, we should not just sit back and do nothing. We are meant to fight off whatever is making us less than we should be. And so we might try to intensify our prayer, we

might take on some penance, or we might make a closer examination of ourselves and our life of faith.

[320]   7. Oftentimes in desolation, we feel that God has left us to fend for ourselves. By faith we know that he is always with us in the strength and power of his grace, but at the time of apparent abandonment we are little aware of his care and concern. We experience neither the support nor the sweetness of his love, and our own response lacks fervor and intensity. It is as if we are living a skeletal life of the bare bones of faith.

[321]   8. The important attitude to nourish at a time of desolation is patience. Patience can mitigate the frustration, dryness, or emptiness of the desolation period and so allow us to live through it a little less painfully. We should try to recall that everything has its time, and consolation has been ours in the past and will be God's gift in the future. Patience should mark even the efforts we undertake to work against the desolation which afflicts us.

[322]   9. Three important reasons why we suffer desolation are:

(1) it is our own fault because we have not lived our life of faith with any effort. We have become tepid and slothful and our very shallowness in the spiritual life has brought about the experience of desolation;

(2) it is a trial period allowed by God. We find ourselves tested as to whether we love God or just love his gifts, whether we continue to follow his call in darkness and dryness as well as in light and consolation;

(3) it is a time when God lets us experience our own poverty and need. We see more clearly that the free gift of consolation is not something we can control, buy, or make our own.
Next follow two guidelines dealing with spiritual consolation:

[323]   10. When we are enjoying a consolation period, we should use foresight and savor the strength of such a period against the time when we may no longer find ourselves in consolation.

[324]   11. A time of consolation should provide the opportunity for a growth in true humility. We can acknowledge with gratitude the gifts we have received and recognize the full gratuity of

God's favor. It may be well to take stock how poorly we fare when such consolation is withdrawn.

On the other hand, if we are afflicted by desolation, we should take some consolation in knowing that God's grace is always sufficient to follow the way of the Lord.

Through three images we can understand better
the ways in which the evil spirit works.

12. The evil spirit often behaves like a spoiled child. If a [325] person is firm with such a child, the child gives up his petulant ways. But if a person shows indulgence or weakness in any way, the child is merciless in getting his own way by stomping his feet or by false displays of affection. So our tactics must include firmness in dealing with the evil spirit in our lives.

13. The evil spirit's behavior can also be compared to a false [326] lover. The false lover uses other people for his own selfish ends, and so he uses people like objects at his disposal or as his playthings for entertainments and good times. He usually suggests that the so-called intimacy of the relationship be kept secret because he is afraid that his duplicity will become known. So the evil spirit often acts in order to keep his own suggestions and temptations secret, and our tactics must be to bring out into the light of day such suggestions and temptations to our confessor or director or superior.

14. The evil spirit can also work like a shrewd army com- [327] mander, who carefully maps out the tactics of attack at weak points of the defense. He knows that weakness is found in two ways: (a) the weakness of fragility or unpreparedness, and (b) the weakness of complacent strength which is pride. The evil spirit's attacks come against us at both of these points of weakness. The first kind of weakness is less serious in that we more readily acknowledge our need and cry out for help to the Lord. The second kind is far more serious and more devastating in its effect upon us so that it is a more favored tactic of the evil spirit.

[328]   PART II. Guidelines Suitable Especially for the Second Week

The following statements are also meant to be helpful in understanding the interior movements which are a part of our spiritual lives. These guidelines are more subtle than the norms described in PART I because commonly in the progress of a good person's life the direction of all movements appears to be towards God and the proper development of one's spiritual life. These norms are especially helpful when a person experiences certain movements that commonly occur to persons engaged in the Second Week of the Exercises or thereafter.

A. A Statement of General Application

[329]   1. When we are trying to follow the call of the Lord in our life, we will find that the good spirit tends to give support, encouragement, and oftentimes even a certain delight in all our endeavors.

The evil spirit generally acts to bring about the opposite reaction. The evil spirit will subtly arouse a dissatisfaction with our own efforts, will raise up doubts and anxieties about God's love or our own response, or sting the conscience with thoughts of pride in our attempt to lead a good life.

B. Particular Statements about Consolation

First, consolation is described in terms of its sources.

[330]   2. God alone can bring about consolation without any concomitant causes. We know the experience of having certain thoughts, achievements, or events which bring about a feeling of great consolation in our lives. We also know the effect of another person or persons whose very presence or conversation can give us joy. But we can more readily attribute our consolation directly to the touch of God when there is no thought, no event, no person—in general, no object of any sort—which seems to be the source of such a movement. The directness of sense words, such as "a touch" or "a taste," seems to point more accurately the way to describe this special action of God in our lives. The effect of such a taste or touch, which may bring along delight or joy, is what we can more readily grasp and speak about. But in these cases, we should be aware that God himself is truly said to be the direct source of all our consolation.

3. When there is a reason for consolation, whether it be from   [331]
certain thoughts or achievements or events, or even more so from
certain people who have an effect upon us, then either the good
spirit or the evil spirit can be involved. On the other hand, the
good spirit brings about such consolation in order to strengthen
and to speed the progress of our life in Christ. The evil spirit,
on the other hand, arouses good feelings so that we are drawn
to focus our attention on wrong things, or to pursue a more selfish
motivation, or to find our own will before all else. Quietly and
slowly the change is brought about until the evil direction becomes clear.

Ways of working with spurious consolation are:

4. For a person striving to lead a good life, the evil spirit   [332]
ordinarily begins like an angel of light. For example, we find
ourselves inspired by pious thoughts or holy desires, and then
after some time we are caught up in the pride of our own intel-
lect and in the selfishness of our own desires.

5. We can become discerning persons by examining carefully   [333]
our own experiences. If in reflecting on the course of our
thoughts or our actions we find that from beginning to end our
eyes have remained fixed on the Lord, we can be sure that the
good spirit has been moving us. But if what started off well in our
thought and action begins to be self-focused or to turn us from
our way to God, we should suspect that the evil spirit has somehow twisted the good beginning to an evil direction, and possibly even to an evil end. So we can discover that an original
good course has led us to be weakened spiritually or even to
become desolate or confused. The signs of desolation give clear
indication of the evil spirit's influence.

6. When we recognize that we have been duped by the evil   [334]
spirit through a certain thought progression or course of action,
we should review carefully all the stages which we passed through
from the time when the evil became apparent back to its very
beginnings in the good. By means of such a review, we will find
that we can more quickly catch ourselves when we are being

led on by the deceit of the evil spirit and so we are more en-
abled to guard ourselves in the future.

Finally, there are further insights in regard to
consolation in the progress of our spiritual life:

[335]   7. As we continue to make progress in the spiritual life, the
movement of the good spirit is very delicate, gentle, and often
delightful. It may be compared to the way a drop of water
penetrates a sponge.

When the evil spirit tries to interrupt our progress, the movement is violent, disturbing, and confusing. It may be compared
to the way a waterfall hits a stone ledge below.

In persons whose lives are going from bad to worse, the descriptions given above should just be reversed. The reason for
this lies in the conflict of opposing forces. In other words, when
good or evil spirits find our heart a true haven, they enter quietly
just as anyone comes into his own home. By contrast, evil spirits
cause great commotion and noise as they try to enter into the
heart of the just person intent upon the good.

[336]   8. When the consolation experience in our life comes directly
from God, there can be no deception in it. Although a delight
and a peace will be found in such an experience, a spiritual person should be very careful to distinguish the actual moment of
this consolation-in-God-himself from the afterglow which may
be exhilarating and joyful for some period of time. Quite often
it is in this second period of time, that we begin to reason out
plans of action or to make resolutions which cannot be attributed
so directly to God as the initial experience which is non-con-
ceptual in nature. Because human reasoning and other influences are now coming into the total picture of this consolation
period, a very careful process of discerning the good and the
evil spirits should be undertaken according to the previous guidelines before any resolution or plan of action is adopted.

OF ONE'S WEALTH AND POSSESSIONS

Preliminary Note: St. Ignatius of Loyola wrote these guidelines as a help for a special group of retreatants who played a most important part in the Christian society of his day. These people had certain responsibilities to the poor and needy because of ecclesiastical benefices or specified inheritances. They faced special obligations in the area of Christian charity because of their office or ministry.

Even though the particular ministry of distributing alms was the historical stimulus to Ignatius' guidelines, we can still find helpful the attitudes which he proposes for our own Christian sharing with those in need today.

In our Christian sharing of our own wealth and resources, the following guidelines are meant to be helpful:

1. Our first concern should be about ourselves and the way   [344] we live. We should try to live modestly by simplifying our lifestyle as much as possible and by becoming more aware of being thrifty in our use of our world's resources. We should try to image in our lives the attitudes and way of living which we see in Jesus Christ, our model, guide, and Lord.

Historically we have the example of the Third Church Council of Carthage, at which St. Augustine was present. This Council made the decree that the bishop, after the manner of Christ our High Priest, should make himself a model of true Christian living, by observing a simple life-style, especially in terms of his possessions.

In a similar way, all Christian men and women should adapt this kind of simplicity in their life style, according to their office and position in the society in which they live.

By a pious tradition, we have the example of Mary's parents, St. Joachim and St. Anne. They divided what they possessed in three ways. The first part they gave to the poor. The second they divided for the upkeep and services of the Temple. And the third they used for their own support.

[338]   When I consider sharing what I have with those to whom I have some natural obligations, such as family relations, friends, or those persons who hold a certain place in my heart, there are certain criteria to be followed. Some of these were mentioned when we considered the Choice of a State or Way of Life (see [169] above).

1. The love that moves me to want to share with these people for whom I have an affection should be grounded in my love of God our Lord. It is the love of God that moves and stimulates me to express my care and affection in the very sharing of what I have. I should be aware that deeper down than the stimulus which comes from my natural feeling and concern I am moved by God, and he is the source for my being able to love these people ever more fully.

[339]   2. In order to maintain better a certain objectivity in regard to the people for whom I feel affection and with whom I want to share what I have, I place myself in an imaginary relationship with a person whom I have never seen or known. He has a certain responsibility to share what he has, and I want him to be able to do this as well as he can according to his way of life. When I consider the measure of sharing which this person does because he is moved by his love of the Lord, I discover a proper mean for myself and I should act on it. As a result, according to the standard which I rejoice in seeing this person observe, I find my own rule of action.

[340]   3. Another help in reaching objectivity in regard to the people for whom I feel affection and with whom I want to share what I have is found in the consideration of my own death. If I picture myself at the hour of my death, I can ponder what norm I would like to have observed in fulfilling my responsibilities of Christian charity. This norm I will take upon myself now and observe it in my attempts to share the goods which I call my own.

[341]   4. Another help can be the consideration of my own personal judgment before the Lord on the day of my death. I can well imagine what account I would like to give to the Lord in the area of carrying out my Christian responsibilities of charity.

The same way of acting which I would want to be true on judgment day I can now begin to observe and live out.

The preceding four criteria are meant to help me when I feel [342] moved to share what I have because of the natural inclinations and affection which I find within myself. I should test my freedom from all disordered attachments by these criteria. I should not begin to share my goods until I can feel myself free to act, no longer under the influence of any disordered attachment.

When it is a matter of my own job or position bringing me [343] into the responsibility of distributing money or goods, I may find that God truly calls me to this way of life. The danger may lie in the manner in which I execute this job or office—using the funds and resources to my own enhancement, comfort, and privilege. I should look to the criteria already given in order that I might better fulfill my God-given responsibility.

351]   St. Ignatius of Loyola was troubled severely by scruples in
the early Manresan days (1522-1523) of his conversion. His
notes about scruples undoubtedly come from his own experience as well as from his attempt to help others. In the light of
modern psychology and pastoral counseling, there is a certain
naiveté present in these notes. Perhaps Ignatius' own nonde-
script title of "Notes" indicates the less than definitive nature
of these reflections. Although some help can still be derived
from these notes, there seemed to be less purpose in rendering
them in a more contemporary style. Instead, the following observations are made, along with some further reading references.

1. The traditional approach to scrupulosity, represented
soundly enough in St. Ignatius' Notes, was quick to identify the
problem as a direct trial inflicted by the devil or a special prob-
ing by God for his own spiritual purposes. Today with the help
provided by modern psychology and psychiatry, most experienced spiritual directors would agree that there is a greater
complexity in clarifying the experience of scrupulosity.

2. Until very recently confessors were often encouraged to
become the conscience for the person who is afflicted by scruples. Presently scruples are not seen so exclusively as an ailment
of our conscience. For in many cases when we are suffering
from scruples, we know what is objectively right or wrong and
so our conscience is functioning quite well. The real problem
in this instance lies more in the emotional area which paralyzes
us and prevents us from applying our correct conclusions to ourselves with any degree of comfort.

3. Commonly, scruples are rooted in the emotion of fear—a
general anxiety about leading the good life or a fixed anxiety
about one area of life such as the sexual. Scruples arising from
a neurotic compulsion also take on varying forms in people—
compulsion over the letter of the law in general or compulsion
in regard to one small area of legal perfection.

4. Scrupulosity, rooted as it is more within our emotions than in our judgment, needs the help of a person experienced in counseling. With such help we can begin to uncover the roots of our emotional disturbance and so start to work with and integrate these experiences of scrupulosity. If the case of scruples is acute, the aid of a psychologist or psychiatrist is recommended.

5. Spiritual literature makes us aware of another phenomenon. In the development of our spiritual life, there can be a true awakening of conscience to a wholly new delicacy of conscience. If we have been living at a certain superficial level of security or certainty about the quality of our Christian faith, we are shaken out of that complacency by some kind of strong religious experience.

Properly speaking, the temporary lack of certitude and firmness of judgment aroused by this experience is not scrupulosity. Instead, this is recognized traditionally as a symptom of growth —a period of time when we need careful guidance to grow in our response to God's call. We desire to move beyond the now-recognized dullness or obtuseness of our conscience because we are roused by a new sensitivity of love.

6. Both in the case of scruples properly so called and in the case of a person being awakened to a true God-given delicacy of conscience, the support, patience, and encouragement of a confessor or spiritual director is most helpful.

7. The experience of scrupulosity in our life can be integrated like any other apparently harmful or personally diminishing experience. Insofar as it is integrated, we further our spiritual growth and maturity, and we also come to a new delicacy of conscience.

Further References
Bernard Häring, C.Ss.R., *Shalom: Peace. The Sacrament of Reconciliation* (New York: Farrer, Straus, and Giroux, 1967), pp. 294-299.
Norman Camerson, Ph.D., *Personality Development and Psychopathology* (Boston: Houghton Mifflin Company, 1963), pp. 373-411.

GUIDELINES ON THINKING WITH THE CHURCH TODAY

Preliminary Note. St. Ignatius of Loyola was convinced that the man or woman who makes the thirty day Exercises would be taking on a more active and concerned role in the life of the Church. In the midst of the confusion and turmoil of the sixteenth-century Church of his day, he knew the difficulty of maintaining a mature balance, a clear-headed judgment, and a loving reverence for both tradition and change. The guidelines which he proposed were meant to be internalized by the retreatant, just as the Guidelines with regard to Eating or the Guidelines for the Discernment of Spirits. In this way, a person could come more easily to responsible judgment and action in everyday life. Even though Ignatius' statements were made in the light of events in the Church of his day, the elements which he includes in his reflections have a lasting value for our own behavior.

The following statements are meant to be helpful in developing a true and loving sensitivity to the ways of thinking, feeling, and acting as a Catholic in our present-day Church.

[353]   1. When legitimate authority speaks within the Church, we should listen with receptive ears and be more prompt to respond favorably than to criticize in a condemnatory way.

[354]   2. We should praise and reverence the sacramental life in the Church, especially encouraging a more personal involvement and a more frequent participation in the celebration of the Eucharist and of the sacrament of reconciliation.

[355]   3. We should praise and reverence the prayer life in the Church, especially as it has been developed in the Eucharistic celebration and in the public morning and evening praise service of the Divine Office.

[356]   4. We should praise and esteem all vocations as God-given within the Church—married life, the dedicated single life, the priestly life, and the religious life.

5. We should praise the religiously vowed life of poverty, [357] chastity, and obedience as the special sign of God's call to a Kingdom whose value system stands in contrast to the value system of our world.

6. We should have a loving reverence for all the men and [358] women who have gone before us and make up the communion of saints, especially those whom the Church has identified as helpers for us in our own struggling lives here and now. Our prayers for their support and our various devotions are our living out of the mystery that we all form the one communion of saints and that there is a continuing concern of all the members for one another.

7. We should respect the Christian call to penance and should [359] respond freely to the abstinence and fasting of the prescribed days in the Church year. We should also continue our personal search for ways of giving expression to the carrying of our cross daily in our following of Jesus Christ.

8. We should show respect for our places of worship and for [360] the statues, paintings, and decorations which are an attempt to beautify them and help us in praising God.

9. The law and precepts within the Church are meant to be of [361] help for the institutional life of the Body of Christ. As a result, we should maintain a proper respect for such laws and respond full-heartedly to them for the good order of the whole Body.

10. We should be more ready to give our support and appro- [362] val to our leaders, both in their personal conduct and in their directives, than to find fault with them. Only greater dissatis-faction and disunity among us is caused by public criticism and defamation of character. Rather the proper steps in remedying a wrong, harmful, unjust, or scandalous situation would be to refer and make representation to the persons who can do some-thing about the problem.

11. We should praise and respect the work of the theologians [363] in our Church, especially those who have given us the legacy of positive and scholastic doctrine. Some men, such as St. Jerome, St. Augustine, and St. Gregory, have given us their theological reflections in a way that we are moved to a greater love and service of God. Today, too, some theologians write in

this more devotional way. Others, such as St. Thomas Aquinas, St. Bonaventure, and Peter Lombard (the Master of the Sentences), define and explain doctrine in order to clarify Christian mysteries through analogies and to expose error and fallacious thinking. Some theologians today continue this process, and their writings are often more difficult and less appealing than the first group mentioned. But both kinds of theologians are important for the reflective life of the Church. The modern theologians have this advantage: Moved and enlightened by the grace of God, they have not only the legacy of the men before them and the rich development of Scripture studies, but also very importantly the whole tradition of the official Church's teaching as summed up in Church Councils, decrees, and constitutions up to the present time.

[364]   12. We sometimes act as if we have discovered Christianity and true holiness for the first time in our own day. And so we have the tendency to exaggerate the contribution of a particular person in our contemporary Church or the holiness of life exemplified in certain practices. We should avoid making comparisons which attempt to exalt some of our own present-day leaders and practices at the expense of past peoples and traditions.

[365]   13. We believe that Christ our Lord has shared his Spirit with the Church in a lasting way. The Spirit, then, is present in the whole Church and its leaders, and continues the influence and guidance which her leadership gives to all the faithful. Although there may be matters which we as individuals at times cannot see or grasp, the Church may have given some direction about it in order to aid us in our Christian life. In the area of the infallibility of the dogmas defined by the Church, we must surrender our own private judgment. We should be more open to acknowledge the limitations of our own individual opinion than to scorn the light of the Spirit's action within the tradition and communal vision of a Church which is described as truly catholic.

[366]   14. It will always remain difficult to describe adequately the saving will of God. That God wants all men to be saved is revealed. That man has the freedom to reject God in a decisive way is also our belief. We should be careful in our thinking and speaking about this matter not to begin to deny either of these two essential statements of our Christian faith.

15. Because we must work out our salvation through our whole [367] lifetime by the grace of God, we must avoid the two following extremes. Being pessimistic to the point of despair, we could act as if we have no ability to act freely or to change and so we deny the God-given gift of our personal freedom as well as the power of his grace, with which we must cooperate. Or being presumptuous, we could act as if we ourselves can change and grow and become perfect solely through our own efforts, with God and his grace being incidental to our salvation.

16. From what has been said above, there is always the danger [368] of so stressing the importance of faith in God and his grace for our salvation that we ignore the necessity of living out lives of active love for our neighbor and for our world.

17. Similarly, we can so stress the power of grace that we can [369] be remiss in taking the human means to remedy physical, psychological, and spiritual evils. We must not try to escape from the responsibility to use our freedom and to choose from all the various means for our growth and development which God has given us in our contemporary world.

18. Today we have a great emphasis on the motivation of love [370] being central to our Christian lives. Yet we can so overstress a language of love, that we ignore the value of Christian fear—the fear of the Lord which acknowledges God as God and the filial fear of offending a Father who loves us. And so in the practical living of our Christian lives, we must acknowledge and make use of the various motivating factors which lead us on in our growth and development.

GENERAL INDEX

to

St. Ignatius' book of *Spiritual Exercises*